1 April 2004

Gordon;

    To the man who enjoys preparing
some delicious soups... Here are more
ideas. Love on the occasion of our "37th"
anniversary.

        Laura.

The soup
bible

The soup bible

All the soups
you could ever
need in one
inspiring
collection

Consultant Editor
DEBRA MAYHEW

HERMES
HOUSE

This edition published by Hermes House in 2003

© Anness Publishing Limited 1999, 2003

Hermes House is an imprint of
Anness Publishing Limited
Hermes House, 88–89 Blackfriars Road, London SE1 8HA
info@anness.com

A CIP catalogue record for this book is available from the British Library

Publisher: Joanna Lorenz; *Editor:* Debra Mayhew;
Production Controller: Ann Childers; *Editorial Reader:* Hayley Kerr
Designer: Bill Mason; *Illustrator:* Anna Koska.

Recipe Contributors: Catherine Atkinson, Alex Barker, Michelle Berriedale-Johnson, Anglela Boggiano,
Janet Brinkworth, Carla Capalbo, Kit Chan, Jacqueline Clark, Maxine Clark, Frances Cleary,
Carole Clements, Andi Clevely, Trish Davies, Roz Denny, Patrizia Diemling, Matthew Drennan,
Sarah Edmonds, Joanna Farrow, Rafi Fernandez, Christine France, Sarah Gates, Shirley Gill,
Rosamund Grant, Rebekah Hassan, Deh-Ta Hsiung, Shehzad Husain, Judy Jackson, Sheila Kimberley,
Masaki Ko, Elisabeth Lambert Ortiz, Ruby Le Bois, Gilly Love, Lesley Mackley, Norma MacMillan,
Sue Maggs, Kathy Man, Sallie Morris, Annie Nichols, Maggie Pannell, Katherine Richmond, Anne
Sheasby, Jenny Stacey, Liz Trigg, Hilaire Walden, Laura Washburn, Steven Wheeler, Kate Whiteman,
Elizabeth Wolf-Cohen, Jeni Wright.

Photographers: Karl Adamson, Edward Allwright, David Armstrong, Steve Baxter, James Duncan,
John Freeman, Ian Garlic, Michelle Garrett, Amanda Heywood, Janine Hosegood, David Jordan,
William Lingwood, Patrick McLeary, Michael Michaels, Thomas Odulate, Juliet Piddington, Peter Reilly.

1 3 5 7 9 10 8 6 4 2

NOTES
For all recipes, quantities are given in both metric and imperial measures and, where appropriate,
measures are also given in standard cups and spoons.
Follow one set, but not a mixture, because they are not interchangeable.

Standard spoon and cup measurements are level: *1 tbsp = 15ml, 1 tsp = 5ml, 1 cup = 250ml/8fl oz*

Australian standard tablespoons are 20ml. Australian readers should use 3 tsp in place of 1 tbsp for
measuring small quantities of gelatine, cornflour, salt, etc.

Medium eggs should be used unless otherwise stated.

CONTENTS

Introduction

YOU WILL FIND PLENTY in these pages to inspire you: cold, light soups to refresh your palate on a hot summer's day; rich and creamy soups to slide like velvet over your taste buds; spicy soups to warm and comfort you on a cold winter's day; and hearty soups, full of goodness, to provide a satisfying lunch when hunger strikes. Here, in one collection, are soups for any occasion.

Few dishes give more all-round pleasure than a good home-made soup, so it is hardly surprising that some soups feature in every cuisine around the world – as readers of this book will discover – whether they are called gumbos, potages, broths, chowders or consommées. Now that once-unfamiliar ingredients are readily available in specialist food shops and many supermarkets, the world of soups is yours to explore.

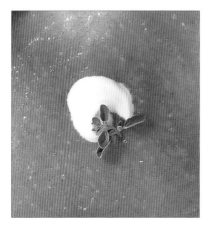

Visit continental Europe and sample diverse delights such as the filling Pistou from France, cooling Gazpacho from Spain or warming Lentil and Bacon Soup from Germany. Try a traditional Smoked Haddock and Potato Soup from the British Isles or fruity soups from central Europe, like Romania's Apple Soup, or classic Borscht from Russia. Be tempted by soups from the African continent such as Chicken Soup with

Vermicelli from Morocco or Smoked Cod and Okra Soup from Ghana. The East beckons with piquant and translucent soups, such as the traditional Hot and Sour Soup from China and the stunning Prawn Ball and Egg Knot Soup from Japan. Make sure you don't miss the USA's Sausage and Seafood Gumbo or Mexico's Jalapeño-style Soup with chicken, chilli and avocado.

Good soup is easy to make, especially if you take care to choose the freshest ingredients, especially those in season. A good stock is necessary as the basis for many – though by no means all – soups. This takes time to make, but large quantities can be prepared in advance and frozen in smaller portions to await a bout of soup making at your convenience. Recipes for basic vegetable, fish, meat, poultry, Chinese and Japanese stocks are given in the following pages.

The right garnish, too, enhances even the simplest soup; giving careful thought to the presentation of your soup adds a professional finish. Herby croûtons or crunchy leek haystacks, for example, arranged in the centre of your soup adds a contrasting texture and a complementary flavour. Try out the suggested garnishes in this book, then have fun developing your own perfect finishes.

Each soup recipe in this collection features step-by-step instructions, many illustrated, to guide you through the soup-making process. Beautiful colour pictures show the finished dish. So take your time to try out many of the delicious recipes featured here. You will soon grow in confidence and begin to change the basic recipes here and there to create your own personalized favourites.

Those who do not eat meat or fish should look for the special symbol $\boxed{V}$ beside a recipe which indicates that it is suitable for vegetarians. These recipes contain no meat or fish products but do contain cheese; vegetarian varieties of cheese can be substituted where desired. A recipe for a vegetarian version of Japanese *Dashi* is suggested alongside the traditional version. In addition, many of the vegetable or bean soups use chicken stock, which can easily be replaced with a vegetable version.

If you have yet to experience the satisfaction gained from making and eating your own soup at home, or if you are an experienced soup maker and want to increase your repertoire of recipes, you need look no further than the pages of this beautifully-illustrated book for inspiration. Turn the page and savour the recipes.

Making your own stocks

Fresh stocks are indispensable for creating good home-made soups. They add a depth of flavour that plain water just cannot achieve.

Although many supermarkets now sell tubs of fresh stock, these can work out expensive, especially if you need large quantities for your cooking. Making your own is surprisingly easy and much more economical, particularly if you can use leftovers – the chicken carcass from Sunday lunch, for example, or the shells you're left with once you've peeled prawns.

But home-made stocks aren't just cheaper, they're also a lot tastier and they're much more nutritious too, precisely because they're made with fresh, natural ingredients.

You can, of course, use stock cubes or granules, but be sure to check the seasoning as these tend to be particularly high in salt.

One good idea for keen and regular soup makers is to freeze home-made stock in plastic freezer bags, or ice cube trays, so you always have a supply at your disposal whenever you need some.

Frozen stock can be stored in the freezer for up to six months. Ensure that you label each stock carefully for easy identification.

Use the appropriate stock for the soup you are making. Onion soup, for example, is improved with a good beef stock. Be particularly careful to use a vegetable stock if you are catering for vegetarians.

Recipes are given on the following pages for vegetable stock, chicken stock, meat stock, fish stock and basic stocks for Chinese and Japanese cooking.

Vegetable Stock

Use this versatile stock as the basis for all vegetarian soups.

INGREDIENTS

Makes 2.5 litres/4½ pints/11 cups

2 leeks, roughly chopped

3 celery sticks, roughly chopped

1 large onion, with skin, chopped

2 pieces fresh root ginger, chopped

1 yellow pepper, seeded and chopped

1 parsnip, chopped

mushroom stalks

tomato peelings

45 ml/3 tbsp light soy sauce

3 bay leaves

a bunch of parsley stalks

3 sprigs of fresh thyme

1 sprig of fresh rosemary

10 ml/2 tsp salt

freshly ground black pepper

3.5 litres/6 pints/15 cups cold water

1 Put all the ingredients into a very large saucepan. Bring slowly to the boil, then lower the heat and simmer for 30 minutes, stirring from time to time.

2 Allow to cool. Strain, then discard the vegetables. The stock is ready to use. Alternatively, chill or freeze the stock and keep it to use as required.

Fish Stock

Fish stock is much quicker to make than poultry or meat stock. Ask your fishmonger for heads, bones and trimmings from white fish.

INGREDIENTS

Makes about 1 litre/ 1³/₄ pints/4 cups

675 g/1¹/₂ lb heads, bones and trimmings
    from white fish
1 onion, sliced
2 celery sticks with leaves, chopped
1 carrot, sliced
¹/₂ lemon, sliced (optional)
1 bay leaf
a few sprigs of fresh parsley
6 black peppercorns
1.35 litres/2¹/₄ pints/6 cups cold water
150 ml/¹/₄ pint/²/₃ cup dry white wine

1　Rinse the fish heads, bones and trimmings well under cold running water. Put in a stockpot with the vegetables and lemon, if using, the herbs, peppercorns, water and wine. Bring to the boil, skimming the surface frequently, then reduce the heat and simmer for 25 minutes.

2　Strain the stock without pressing down on the ingredients in the sieve. If not using immediately, leave to cool and then refrigerate. Fish stock should be used within 2 days, or it can be frozen for up to 3 months.

Chicken Stock

A good home-made poultry stock is invaluable in the kitchen. If poultry giblets are available, add them (except the livers) with the wings. Once made, chicken stock can be kept in an airtight container in the refrigerator for 3–4 days, or frozen for longer storage (up to 6 months).

INGREDIENTS

Makes about 2.5 litres/4 ½ pints/11 cups

1.2–1.5 kg/2½–3 lb chicken or turkey
   (wings, backs and necks)
2 onions, unpeeled, quartered
1 tbsp olive oil
4 litres/7 pints/17½ cups cold water
2 carrots, roughly chopped
2 celery sticks, with leaves if possible,
   roughly chopped
a small handful of fresh parsley
a few sprigs of fresh thyme or
   3.5 ml/¾ tsp dried thyme
1 or 2 bay leaves
10 black peppercorns, lightly crushed

1 Combine the poultry wings, backs and necks in a stockpot with the onion quarters and the oil. Cook over moderate heat, stirring occasionally, until the poultry and onions are lightly and evenly browned.

2 Add the water and stir well to mix in the sediment on the bottom of the pan. Bring to the boil and skim off the impurities as they rise to the surface of the stock.

3 Add the chopped carrots and celery, fresh parsley, thyme, bay leaf and black peppercorns. Partly cover the stockpot and gently simmer the stock for about 3 hours.

4 Strain the stock through a sieve into a bowl and leave to cool, then chill in the refrigerator for an hour.

5 When cold, carefully remove the layer of fat that will have set on the surface. Store in the refrigerator for 3–4 days or freeze until required.

Meat Stock

The most delicious meat soups rely on a good home-made stock for success. A stock cube will do if you do not have time to make your own. Once it is made, meat stock can be kept in the refrigerator for 4–5 days, or frozen for longer storage.

INGREDIENTS

Makes about 2 litres/3¹/₂ pints/9 cups

1.75 kg/4 lb beef bones, such as shin, leg,
   neck and shank, or veal or lamb bones,
   cut into 6 cm/2¹/₂ in pieces
2 onions, unpeeled, quartered
2 carrots, roughly chopped
2 celery sticks, with leaves if possible,
   roughly chopped
2 tomatoes, coarsely chopped
4.5 litres/7¹/₂ pints/20 cups cold water
a handful of parsley stalks
few sprigs of fresh thyme or
   3.5 ml/³/₄ tsp dried thyme
2 bay leaves
10 black peppercorns, lightly crushed

1   Preheat the oven to 230°C/ 450°F/Gas 8. Put the bones in a roasting tin and roast, turning occasionally, for 30 minutes until they start to brown.

2   Add the onions, carrots, celery and tomatoes and baste with the fat in the tin. Roast for a further 20–30 minutes until the bones are well browned. Stir and baste occasionally.

3   Transfer the bones and roasted vegetables to a stockpot. Spoon off the fat from the roasting tin. Add a little of the water to the roasting tin or casserole and bring to the boil on top of the stove, stirring well to scrape up any browned bits. Pour this liquid into the stockpot.

4   Add the remaining water to the pot. Bring just to the boil, skimming frequently to remove all the foam from the surface. Add the parsley, thyme, bay leaves and peppercorns.

5   Partly cover the stockpot and simmer the stock for 4–6 hours. The bones and vegetables should always be covered with liquid, so top up with a little boiling water from time to time if necessary.

6   Strain the stock through a colander, then skim as much fat as possible from the surface. If possible, cool the stock and then refrigerate it; the fat will rise to the top and set in a layer that can be removed easily.

Stock for Chinese Cooking

This stock is an excellent basis for soup making.

INGREDIENTS

Makes 2.5 litres/4¹/₂ pints/11 cups
675 g/1¹/₂ lb chicken portions
675 g/1¹/₂ lb pork spareribs
3.75 litres/6 pints/16 cups cold water
3–4 pieces fresh root ginger, unpeeled, crushed
3–4 spring onions, each tied into a knot
45–60 ml/3–4 tbsp Chinese rice wine or dry sherry

1 Trim off any excess fat from the chicken and spareribs and chop them into large pieces.

2 Place the chicken and sparerib pieces into a large stockpot with the water. Add the ginger and spring onion knots.

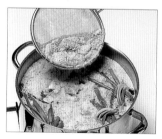

3 Bring to the boil and, using a sieve, skim off the froth. Reduce the heat and simmer, uncovered, for about 2–3 hours.

4 Strain the stock, discarding the chicken, pork, ginger and spring onions. Add the wine or sherry and return to the boil. Simmer for 2–3 minutes. Refrigerate the stock when cool. It will keep for up to 4–5 days. Alternatively, it can be frozen in small containers and defrosted when required.

Stock for Japanese Cooking

Dashi *is the stock that gives the characteristically Japanese flavour to many dishes. Known as* Ichiban-dashi, *it is used for delicately flavoured dishes, including soups. Of course instant stock is available in all Japanese supermarkets, either in granule form, in concentrate or even in a tea-bag style. Follow the instructions on the packet.*

INGREDIENTS

Makes about 800 ml/1¹/₃ pints/3¹/₂ cups

10 g/¹/₄ oz dried kombu seaweed

10–15 g/¹/₄–¹/₂ oz bonito flakes

VARIATION
∽

For vegetarian dashi, just omit the bonito flakes (dried tuna) and follow the same method.

1 Wipe the kombu seaweed with a damp cloth and cut two slits in it with scissors, so that it flavours the stock effectively.

2 Soak the kombu in 900 ml/ 1¹/₂ pints/3³/₄ cups cold water for 30–60 minutes.

3 Heat the kombu in its soaking water over a moderate heat. Just before the water boils, remove the seaweed. Then add the bonito flakes and bring to the boil over a high heat, then remove the pan from the heat.

4 Leave the stock until all the bonito flakes have sunk to the bottom of the pan. Line a strainer with kitchen paper or muslin and place it over a large mixing bowl, then gently strain the stock.

Garnishes

Sometimes, a soup needs something to lift it out of the ordinary, and garnishes are the answer. They are an important finishing touch, bringing that little extra to soups; they not only look good but also add an extra dimension to the flavour. A garnish can be as simple as a sprinkling of chopped parsley, a swirl of cream or some freshly grated cheese. Alternatively, it can be something that requires a little more attention, such as home-made croûtons or sippets. All the garnishes featured here are suitable for vegetarians.

DUMPLINGS

These dumplings are easy to make and add an attractive and tasty finishing touch to country soups.

INGREDIENTS

75 g/3 oz/¹/₂ cup semolina or flour
1 egg, beaten
45 ml/3 tbsp milk or water
a generous pinch of salt
15 ml/1 tbsp chopped fresh parsley

1 Mix all the ingredients together into a soft, elastic dough. Leave to stand, covered with clear film, for 5–10 minutes.

2 Drop small rounded dessert-spoonfuls of this mixture into the soup and cook for 10 minutes until firm.

CRISPY CROÛTONS

Croûtons add a lovely crunchy texture to creamy soups and are a good way of using up stale bread. Use thinly sliced ciabatta or French bread for delicious results.

INGREDIENTS

bread
good quality, flavourless oil, such as sunflower or groundnut or, for a fuller flavour, extra-virgin olive oil or a flavoured oil such as one with garlic and herbs or chilli

1 Preheat the oven to 200°C/400°F/Gas 6. Cut the bread into small cubes and place on a baking sheet.

2 Brush with your chosen oil, then bake for about 15 minutes until golden and crisp. Allow to start to cool: they crisp up further as they cool down.

3 Store them in an airtight container for up to a week. Reheat in a warm oven, if liked, before serving.

RIVELS

Rivels are pea-size pieces of dough which swell when cooked in a soup.

INGREDIENTS

1 egg
75–115 g/3–4 oz/³/₄–1 cup flour
2.5 ml/¹/₂ tsp salt
freshly ground black pepper

1 Beat the egg in a bowl. Add the flour, salt and pepper to taste and mix with a wooden spoon. Finish mixing with your fingers, rubbing to blend the egg and flour together to form pea-size pieces.

2 Bring the soup back to the boil. Sprinkle in the pieces of dough, stirring gently.

3 Reduce the heat and simmer for about 6 minutes, until the rivels are slightly swollen and cooked through. Serve at once.

SWIRLED CREAM

A swirl of cream is the classic finish for many soups, such as a smooth tomato soup and chilled asparagus soup. The garnish gives a professional finish to your soup, although the technique is simplicity itself.

INGREDIENTS

single cream

1 Transfer the cream into a jug with a good pouring lip. Pour a swirl on to the surface of each bowl of soup.

2 Draw the tip of a fine skewer quickly backwards and forwards through the cream to create a delicate pattern. Serve the soup immediately.

SIPPETS

Another good way of using up slightly stale bread, sippets are larger than croûtons and have a more intense flavour because of the addition of fresh herbs. Experiment with the herbs according to the flavour of the soup.

INGREDIENTS

3 slices day-old bread

50 g/2 oz/4 tbsp butter

45 ml/3 tbsp finely chopped fresh parsley, or coriander or basil

1 Cut the bread into fingers about 2.5 cm/1 in long.

2 Melt the butter into a large frying pan, toss in the small fingers of bread and fry gently until golden brown.

3 Add the fresh herbs and stir well to combine. Cook for a further minute, stirring continuously. Strew the sippets on top of the soup and serve.

LEEK HAYSTACKS

Stacks of golden leek look good served on a creamy soup and the crunchy texture contrasts well with the smoothness of the soup.

INGREDIENTS

1 large leek

30 ml/2 tbsp plain flour

oil, for deep frying

1 Slice the leek in half lengthways and then cut into quarters. Cut into 5 cm/2 in lengths and then into very fine strips. Place in a bowl, sprinkle the flour over and toss to coat.

2 Heat the oil to 160ºC/325ºF. Drop small spoonfuls of the floured leeks into the oil and cook for 30–45 seconds until golden. Drain on kitchen paper. Repeat with the remaining leeks.

3 Serve the soup with a small stack of leeks piled on top of each bowl.

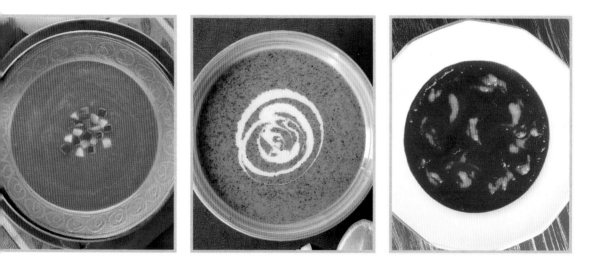

LIGHT &
REFRESHING
SOUPS

~

Chilled Asparagus Soup

This delicate, pale green soup, garnished with a swirl of cream or yogurt, is as pretty as it is delicious.

INGREDIENTS

Serves 6

900 g/2 lb fresh asparagus
60 ml/4 tbsp butter or olive oil
175 g/6 oz/1½ cups sliced leeks or
   spring onions
45 ml/3 tbsp flour
1.5 litres/2½ pints/6¼ cups chicken stock
   or water
120 ml/4 fl oz/½ cup single cream or
   natural yogurt
15 ml/1 tbsp chopped fresh tarragon
   or chervil
salt and freshly ground black pepper

1 Cut the top 6 cm/2½ in off the asparagus spears and blanch the tips in boiling water for 5–6 minutes until just tender. Drain thoroughly. Cut each tip into two or three pieces and set aside.

2 Trim the ends of the stalks, removing any brown or woody parts. Chop the stalks into 1 cm/½ in pieces.

3 Heat the butter or oil in a heavy-based saucepan. Add the sliced leeks or spring onions and cook over a low heat for 5–8 minutes until softened but not browned. Stir in the chopped asparagus stalks, cover and cook for another 6–8 minutes until the stalks are tender.

4 Add the flour and stir well to blend. Cook for 3–4 minutes, uncovered, stirring occasionally.

5 Add the stock or water. Bring to the boil, stirring frequently, then reduce the heat and simmer for 30 minutes. Season with salt and pepper.

6 Purée the soup in a food processor or food mill. If necessary, strain it to remove any coarse fibres. Stir in the asparagus tips, most of the cream or yogurt, and the herbs. Chill well. Stir before serving and check the seasoning. Garnish each bowl with a swirl of cream or yogurt.

Miami Chilled Avocado Soup

Avocados are combined with lemon juice, dry sherry and an optional dash of hot pepper sauce, to make this subtle chilled soup.

INGREDIENTS

Serves 4

2 large or 3 medium ripe avocados

15 ml/1 tbsp fresh lemon juice

75 g/3 oz/¾ cup coarsely chopped
  peeled cucumber

30 ml/2 tbsp dry sherry

25 g/1 oz/¼ cup coarsely chopped spring
  onions, with some of the green stems

475 ml/16 fl oz/2 cups mild-flavoured
  chicken stock

5 ml/1 tsp salt

hot pepper sauce (optional)

natural yogurt or cream, to garnish

1 Cut the avocados in half, remove the stones and peel. Roughly chop the flesh and place in a food processor or blender. Add the lemon juice and process until very smooth.

2 Add the cucumber, sherry and most of the spring onions, reserving a few for the garnish. Process again until smooth.

3 In a large bowl, combine the avocado mixture with the chicken stock. Whisk until well blended. Season with the salt and a few drops of hot pepper sauce, if liked. Cover the bowl and place in the refrigerator to chill thoroughly.

4 To serve, fill individual bowls with the soup. Place a spoonful of yogurt or cream in the centre of each bowl and swirl with a spoon. Sprinkle with the reserved chopped spring onions.

Vichyssoise

Serve this flavourful soup with a dollop of crème fraîche or soured cream and sprinkle with a few snipped fresh chives – or, for special occasions, garnish with a small spoonful of caviar.

INGREDIENTS

Serves 6–8

450 g/1 lb/about 3 large potatoes, peeled and cubed

1.5 litres/2½ pints/6¼ cups chicken stock

350 g/12 oz leeks, trimmed

150 ml/¼ pint/⅔ cup crème fraîche or soured cream

salt and freshly ground black pepper

45 ml/3 tbsp snipped fresh chives, to garnish

1 Put the cubed potatoes and chicken stock in a saucepan or flameproof casserole and bring to the boil. Reduce the heat and simmer for 15–20 minutes.

2 Make a slit along the length of each leek and rinse well under cold running water to wash away any soil. Slice thinly.

VARIATION
〜
To make a low-fat soup, use low-fat fromage frais instead of crème fraîche or soured cream.

3 When the potatoes are barely tender, stir in the leeks. Taste then season with salt and freshly ground black pepper and simmer for 10–15 minutes until both the vegetables are soft, stirring from time to time. If the soup is too thick, thin it down with a little more stock or water.

4 Purée the soup in a blender or food processor. If you prefer a very smooth soup, pass it through a food mill or press through a coarse sieve. Stir in most of the cream, cool and then chill. To serve, ladle into chilled bowls and garnish with a swirl of cream and the snipped chives.

Gazpacho

This is a traditional, chilled Spanish soup, perfect for a summer lunch. Make sure that all the ingredients are in peak condition for the best-flavoured soup.

INGREDIENTS

Serves 6

1 green pepper, seeded and roughly chopped

1 red pepper, seeded and roughly chopped

1/2 cucumber, roughly chopped

1 onion, roughly chopped

1 fresh red chilli, seeded and roughly chopped

450 g/1 lb ripe plum tomatoes, roughly chopped

900 ml/1 1/2 pints/3 3/4 cups passata or tomato juice

30 ml/2 tbsp red wine vinegar

30 ml/2 tbsp olive oil

15 ml/1 tbsp caster sugar

salt and freshly ground black pepper

crushed ice, to garnish (optional)

1 Reserve a small piece of green and red pepper, cucumber and onion. Finely chop these and set aside as a garnish.

2 Process all the remaining ingredients (except the ice) in a blender or food processor until smooth. You may need to do this in batches.

3 Pass the soup through a sieve into a clean glass bowl, pushing it through with a spoon to extract the maximum amount of flavour.

4 Adjust the seasoning and chill. Serve sprinkled with the reserved chopped green and red pepper, cucumber and onion. For an extra special touch, add a little crushed ice to the garnish.

Summer Tomato Soup

The success of this soup depends on having ripe, full-flavoured tomatoes, such as the oval plum variety, so make it when the tomato season is at its peak.

INGREDIENTS

Serves 4

15 ml/1 tbsp olive oil
1 large onion, chopped
1 carrot, chopped
1 kg/2¼ lb ripe tomatoes, quartered
2 garlic cloves, chopped
5 sprigs of fresh thyme, or 1.5 ml/¼ tsp
   dried thyme
4 or 5 sprigs of fresh marjoram, or
   1.5 ml/¼ tsp dried marjoram
1 bay leaf
45 ml/3 tbsp crème fraîche, soured cream
   or natural yogurt, plus a little extra
   to garnish
salt and freshly ground black pepper

1 Heat the olive oil in a large, preferably stainless-steel saucepan or flameproof casserole.

2 Add the onion and carrot and cook over a medium heat for 3–4 minutes until just softened, stirring occasionally.

3 Add the quartered tomatoes, chopped garlic and herbs. Reduce the heat and simmer, covered, for 30 minutes.

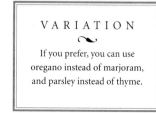

4 Discard the bay leaf and press the soup through a sieve. Stir in the cream or yogurt and season. Leave to cool, then chill in the refrigerator.

VARIATION

If you prefer, you can use oregano instead of marjoram, and parsley instead of thyme.

Watercress and Orange Soup

*This is a healthy and refreshing
soup, which is just as good served
either hot or chilled.*

INGREDIENTS

Serves 4

1 large onion, chopped

15 ml/1 tbsp olive oil

2 bunches or bags of watercress

grated rind and juice of 1 large orange

600 ml/1 pint/2½ cups vegetable stock

150 ml/¼ pint/⅔ cup single cream

10 ml/2 tsp cornflour

salt and freshly ground black pepper

a little thick cream or natural yogurt,
   to garnish

4 orange wedges, to serve

1 Soften the onion in the oil in a
large pan. Add the watercress,
unchopped, to the onion. Cover
and cook for about 5 minutes until
the watercress is softened.

2 Add the orange rind and juice
and the stock to the watercress
mixture. Bring to the boil, cover
and simmer for 10–15 minutes.

3 Blend or liquidize the soup
thoroughly, and sieve if you
want to increase the smoothness of
the finished soup. Blend the cream
with the cornflour until no lumps
remain, then add to the soup.
Season to taste.

4 Bring the soup gently back
to the boil, stirring until just
slightly thickened. Check the
seasoning.

5 Serve the soup with a swirl
of cream or yogurt, and a
wedge of orange to squeeze in
at the last moment.

6 If serving the soup chilled,
thicken as above and leave
to cool, before chilling in the
refrigerator. Garnish with cream
or yogurt and orange, as above.

Chilled Almond Soup

V

Unless you are prepared to spend
time pounding all the ingredients for
this soup by hand, a food processor
is essential. Then you'll find that
this Spanish soup is simple to make
and refreshing to eat on a hot day.

INGREDIENTS

Serves 6

115 g/4 oz fresh white bread
750 ml/1¼ pints/3 cups cold water
115 g/4 oz/1 cup blanched almonds
2 garlic cloves, sliced
75 ml/5 tbsp olive oil
25 ml/1½ tbsp sherry vinegar
salt and freshly ground black pepper

For the garnish

toasted flaked almonds
seedless green and black grapes, halved
   and skinned

1 Break the bread into a bowl
and pour 150 ml/¼ pint/
⅔ cup of the water on top. Leave
for 5 minutes.

2 Put the almonds and garlic in
a blender or food processor
and process until finely ground.
Blend in the soaked bread.

3 Gradually add the oil until the
mixture forms a smooth paste.
Add the sherry vinegar, then the
remaining cold water and process
until smooth.

4 Transfer to a bowl and season
with salt and pepper, adding a
little more water if the soup is too
thick. Chill for at least 2–3 hours.
Serve scattered with the toasted
almonds and grapes.

Cucumber and Yogurt Soup with Walnuts

V

This is a particularly refreshing cold soup, using a classic combination of cucumber and yogurt.

INGREDIENTS

Serves 5–6

1 cucumber

4 garlic cloves

2.5 ml/¹⁄₂ tsp salt

75 g/3 oz/³⁄₄ cup walnut pieces

40 g/1¹⁄₂ oz day-old bread, torn into pieces

30 ml/2 tbsp walnut or sunflower oil

400 ml/14 fl oz/1²⁄₃ cups natural yogurt

120 ml/4 fl oz/¹⁄₂ cup cold water or chilled
   still mineral water

5–10 ml/1–2 tsp lemon juice

For the garnish

40 g/1¹⁄₂ oz/scant ¹⁄₂ cup walnuts,
   coarsely chopped

25 ml/1¹⁄₂ tbsp olive oil

sprigs of fresh dill

3 When the mixture is smooth, slowly add the walnut or sunflower oil and combine well.

4 Transfer the mixture into a large bowl and beat in the yogurt and diced cucumber. Add the cold water or mineral water and lemon juice to taste.

5 Pour the soup into chilled soup bowls to serve. Garnish with the chopped walnuts and drizzle with the olive oil. Finally, arrange the sprigs of dill on top and serve immediately.

COOK'S TIP

If you prefer your soup smooth, purée it in a food processor or blender before serving.

1 Cut the cucumber in half and peel one half of it. Dice the cucumber flesh and set aside.

2 Using a large mortar and pestle, crush together the garlic and salt well, then add the walnuts and bread.

V

Green Pea and Mint Soup

*Perfect partners, peas and mint
really capture the flavours of summer.*

INGREDIENTS

Serves 4

50 g/2 oz/4 tbsp butter

4 spring onions, chopped

450 g/1 lb fresh or frozen peas

600 ml/1 pint/2½ cups vegetable stock

2 large sprigs of fresh mint

600 ml/1 pint/2½ cups milk

a pinch of sugar (optional)

salt and freshly ground black pepper

small sprigs of fresh mint, to garnish

single cream, to serve

1 Heat the butter in a large saucepan, add the chopped spring onions and cook gently on a low heat until they are softened but not browned.

2 Stir the peas into the pan, add the stock and mint, and bring to the boil. Cover and simmer gently for about 30 minutes if you are using fresh peas (15 minutes if you are using frozen peas), until they are tender. Remove about 45 ml/3 tbsp of the peas, and reserve to use for a garnish.

3 Pour the soup into a food processor or blender, add the milk and purée until smooth. Season to taste, adding a pinch of sugar, if liked. Leave to cool, then chill lightly in the refrigerator.

4 Pour the soup into bowls. Swirl a little cream into each, then garnish with the mint and the reserved peas.

Beetroot and Apricot Swirl

This soup is most attractive if you swirl together the two differently coloured mixtures, but if you prefer they can be mixed together to save on both time and washing up.

Serves 4

4 large cooked beetroots, roughly chopped
1 small onion, roughly chopped
600 ml/1 pint/2½ cups chicken stock
200 g/7 oz/1 cup ready-to-eat dried apricots
250 ml/8 fl oz/1 cup orange juice
salt and freshly ground black pepper

2 Place the rest of the onion in a pan with the apricots and orange juice, cover and simmer gently for about 15 minutes, until tender. Purée in a food processor or blender.

3 Return the two mixtures to the saucepans and reheat. Season to taste with salt and pepper, then swirl them together in individual soup bowls for a marbled effect.

1 Place the roughly chopped beetroot and half the onion in a pan with the stock. Bring to the boil, then reduce the heat, cover and simmer for about 10 minutes. Place the mixture in a food processor or blender and purée until smooth.

COOK'S TIP
~

The apricot mixture should be the same consistency as the beetroot mixture – if it is too thick, add a little more orange juice.

Roasted Pepper Soup

Grilling intensifies the flavour of sweet red and yellow peppers and helps this delicious soup to keep its stunning colour.

INGREDIENTS

Serves 4

3 red peppers
1 yellow pepper
1 medium onion, chopped
1 garlic clove, crushed
750 ml/1¼ pints/3 cups vegetable stock
15 ml/1 tbsp plain flour
salt and freshly ground black pepper
diced red and yellow pepper, to garnish

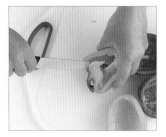

1 Preheat the grill. Cut the peppers in half, remove their stalks, cores and white pith, and scrape out the seeds.

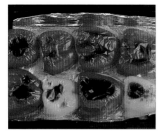

2 Line a grill pan with foil and arrange the halved peppers, skin side up, in a single layer on the foil. Grill until the skins have blackened and blistered.

3 Transfer the peppers to a plastic bag and leave until cool, then peel away their skins and discard. Roughly chop the pepper flesh.

4 Put the onion, garlic clove and 150 ml/¼ pint/⅔ cup of the stock in a large saucepan. Boil for about 5 minutes until the stock has reduced in volume. Reduce the heat and stir until softened and just beginning to colour.

5 Sprinkle the flour over the onion, then gradually stir in the remaining stock.

6 Add the chopped, roasted peppers and bring to the boil. Cover and simmer for a further 5 minutes.

7 Leave to cool slightly, then purée in a food processor or blender until smooth. Season to taste with salt and ground black pepper. Return to the saucepan and reheat until piping hot.

8 Ladle into 4 soup bowls and garnish each with a sprinkling of diced peppers.

VARIATION

If preferred, garnish the soup with a swirl of natural yogurt instead of the diced peppers.

Chicken Stellette Soup

*Simple and quick to prepare,
provided you have some good stock
to hand, this light, clear soup is easy
on the palate and the eye.*

INGREDIENTS

Serves 4–6

900 ml/1½ pints/3¾ cups chicken stock

1 bay leaf

4 spring onions, sliced

225 g/8 oz button mushrooms, sliced

115 g/4 oz cooked chicken breast

50 g/2 oz small soup pasta (stellette)

150 ml/¼ pint/⅔ cup dry white wine

15 ml/1 tbsp chopped parsley

salt and freshly ground black pepper

1 Put the stock and bay leaf into
a large saucepan and bring to
the boil. Add the sliced spring
onions and mushrooms.

2 Remove the skin from the
chicken and discard. Slice the
chicken thinly, add to the soup and
season to taste with salt and pepper.
Heat through for 2–3 minutes.

3 Add the pasta to the soup,
cover and leave to simmer
for 7–8 minutes until the pasta
is *al dente*.

4 Just before serving, add the
wine and chopped parsley and
heat through for 2–3 minutes.
Pour into individual soup bowls.

Courgette Soup with Pasta

*This is a pretty, fresh-tasting soup,
which is always a welcome dish in
hot weather.*

INGREDIENTS

Serves 4–6
60 ml/4 tbsp olive or sunflower oil
2 onions, finely chopped
1.5 litres/2½ pints/6¼ cups chicken stock
900 g/2 1b courgettes
115 g/4 oz small soup pasta (stellette)
a little lemon juice
30 ml/2 tbsp chopped fresh chervil
salt and freshly ground black pepper
soured cream, to serve

1 Heat the oil in a large
saucepan and add the onions.
Cover and cook gently for about
20 minutes, stirring occasionally,
until soft but not coloured.

2 Add the stock to the pan and
bring the mixture to the boil.

3 Meanwhile, grate the
courgettes and stir into the
boiling stock with the pasta.
Reduce the heat, cover the pan and
simmer for 15 minutes until the
pasta is tender.

4 Season to taste with lemon
juice, salt and pepper. Stir
in the chopped fresh chervil.
Pour into bowls and add a swirl
of soured cream before serving.

VARIATION

You can use cucumber instead
of courgettes, if you prefer,
and other soup pasta such as
tiny shells.

Jalapeño-style Soup

Chicken, chilli and avocado combine to make this simple but unusual soup.

INGREDIENTS

Serves 6

1.5 litres/2½ pints/6¼ cups chicken stock
2 cooked chicken breast fillets, skinned
    and cut into large strips
1 drained canned chipotle or jalapeño
    chilli, rinsed
1 avocado

COOK'S TIP

When using canned chillies,
it is important to rinse them
thoroughly before adding them
to a dish so as to remove the
flavour of any pickling liquid.

1 Heat the stock in a large saucepan and add the chicken and chilli. Simmer over a very gentle heat for 5 minutes to heat the chicken through and release the flavour from the chilli.

2 Cut the avocado in half, remove the stone and peel off the skin. Slice the avocado flesh neatly lengthways.

3 Using a slotted spoon, remove the chilli from the stock and discard it. Pour the soup into heated serving bowls, distributing the chicken evenly among them.

4 Carefully add a few avocado slices to each bowl and serve the soup immediately.

Tamarind Soup with Peanuts and Vegetables

Known in Indonesia as Sayur Asam, this is a colourful and refreshing soup from Jakarta with more than a hint of sharpness.

INGREDIENTS

Serves 4 as a starter or 8 as part of a buffet

5 shallots or 1 medium red onion, sliced
3 garlic cloves, crushed
2.5 cm/1 in lengkuas, peeled and sliced
1–2 fresh red chillies, seeded and sliced
25 g/1 oz/¼ cup raw peanuts
1 cm/½ in cube terasi, prepared
1.2 litres/2 pints/5 cups well-flavoured
    stock
50–75 g/2–3 oz/½–¾ cup salted peanuts,
    lightly crushed
15–30 ml/1–2 tbsp dark brown sugar
5 ml/1 tsp tamarind pulp, soaked in
    75 ml/5 tbsp warm water for 15 minutes
salt

For the vegetables

1 chayote, thinly peeled, seeds removed,
    flesh finely sliced
115 g/4 oz French beans, trimmed and
    finely sliced
50 g/2 oz sweetcorn kernels (optional)
a handful of green leaves, such as
    watercress, rocket or Chinese leaves,
    finely shredded
1 fresh green chilli, sliced, to garnish

1 Grind the shallots or onion, garlic, lengkuas, chillies, raw peanuts and terasi to a paste in a food processor, or using a pestle and mortar.

2 Pour in some of the stock to moisten and then pour this mixture into a pan or wok, adding the rest of the stock. Cook for 15 minutes with the crushed salted peanuts and sugar.

3 Strain the tamarind pulp, discarding the seeds, and reserve the juice.

4 About 5 minutes before serving, add the chayote slices, beans and sweetcorn, if using, to the soup and cook fairly rapidly. At the last minute, add the green leaves and salt to taste.

5 Add the tamarind juice and adjust the seasoning. Serve at once, garnished with slices of green chilli.

Spinach and Tofu Soup

This is an extremely delicate and mild-flavoured soup, which can be used to counterbalance the heat from a hot Thai curry.

INGREDIENTS

Serves 4–6

30 ml/2 tbsp dried shrimps
1 litre/1¾ pints/4 cups chicken stock
225 g/8 oz fresh tofu, drained and cut into
    2 cm/¾ in cubes
30 ml/2 tbsp fish sauce
350 g/12 oz fresh spinach
freshly ground black pepper
2 spring onions, finely sliced, to garnish

1 Rinse and drain the dried shrimps. Combine the shrimps with the chicken stock in a large saucepan and bring to the boil. Add the tofu and simmer for about 5 minutes. Season with fish sauce and black pepper to taste.

2 Wash the spinach leaves thoroughly and tear into bite-size pieces. Add to the soup. Cook for another 1–2 minutes.

3 Pour the soup into warmed bowls, sprinkle the chopped spring onions on top to garnish, and serve.

Chinese Tofu and Lettuce Soup

V

This light, clear soup is brimful of colourful, tasty vegetables.

Serves 4

30 ml/2 tbsp groundnut or sunflower oil

200 g/7 oz smoked or marinated tofu, cubed

3 spring onions, sliced diagonally

2 garlic cloves, cut into thin strips

1 carrot, finely sliced into rounds

1 litre/1¾ pints/4 cups vegetable stock

30 ml/2 tbsp soy sauce

15 ml/1 tbsp dry sherry or vermouth

5 ml/1 tsp sugar

115 g/4 oz Cos lettuce, shredded

salt and freshly ground black pepper

1 Heat the oil in a preheated wok, then stir-fry the tofu cubes until browned. Drain on kitchen paper and set aside.

2 Add the spring onions, garlic and carrot to the wok and stir-fry for 2 minutes. Add the stock, soy sauce, sherry or vermouth, sugar, lettuce and fried tofu. Heat through gently for 1 minute, season to taste and serve.

Chinese Chicken and Asparagus Soup

This is a very delicate and delicious soup. When fresh asparagus is not in season, tinned white asparagus is an acceptable substitute.

INGREDIENTS

Serves 4

140 g/5 oz chicken breast fillet
pinch of salt
5 ml/1 tsp egg white
5 ml/1 tsp cornflour paste
115 g/4 oz asparagus
700 ml/1¼ pints/3 cups chicken stock
salt and freshly ground black pepper
fresh coriander leaves, to garnish

1 Cut the chicken meat into thin slices each about the size of a postage stamp. Mix with a pinch of salt, then add the egg white, and finally the cornflour paste.

2 Cut off and discard the tough stems of the asparagus, and diagonally cut the tender spears into short, even lengths.

3 In a wok or saucepan, bring the stock to a rolling boil, add the asparagus and bring back to the boil, cooking for 2 minutes. (You do not need to do this if you are using tinned asparagus.)

4 Add the chicken, stir to separate and bring back to the boil once more. Adjust the seasonings. Serve hot, garnished with fresh coriander leaves.

Hot-and-sour Prawn Soup with Lemon Grass

This classic seafood soup, known as Tom Yam Goong, is probably the most popular and best-known soup from Thailand.

INGREDIENTS

Serves 4–6

450 g/1 lb king prawns

1 litre/1¾ pints/4 cups chicken stock
or water

3 lemon grass stalks

10 kaffir lime leaves, torn in half

225 g/8 oz can straw mushrooms, drained

45 ml/3 tbsp fish sauce

50 ml/2 fl oz/¼ cup lime juice

30 ml/2 tbsp chopped spring onion

15 ml/1 tbsp fresh coriander leaves

4 fresh red chillies, seeded and chopped

2 spring onions, finely chopped,
to garnish

1 Shell and devein the prawns and set aside. Rinse the prawn shells and place in a large saucepan with the stock or water and bring to the boil.

2 Bruise the lemon grass stalks with the blunt edge of a chopping knife and add them to the stock, together with half the lime leaves. Simmer gently for 5–6 minutes until the stalks change colour and the stock is fragrant.

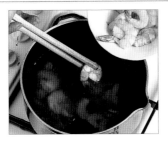

3 Strain the stock, return to the saucepan and reheat. Add the mushrooms and prawns, then cook until the prawns turn pink.

4 Stir in the fish sauce, lime juice, spring onion, coriander, red chillies and the rest of the lime leaves. Taste and adjust the seasoning. The soup should be sour, salty, spicy and hot. Garnish with finely chopped spring onions before serving.

Duck Consommé

The Vietnamese community in France has had a profound influence on French cooking, as this soup bears witness – it is light and rich at the same time, with intriguing flavours of south-east Asia.

INGREDIENTS

Serves 4

1 duck carcass (raw or cooked), plus 2 legs or any giblets, trimmed of as much fat as possible

1 large onion, unpeeled, with root end trimmed

2 carrots, cut into 5 cm/2 in pieces

1 parsnip, cut into 5 cm/2 in pieces

1 leek, cut into 5 cm/2 in pieces

2–4 garlic cloves, crushed

2.5 cm/1 in piece fresh root ginger, peeled and sliced

15 ml/1 tbsp black peppercorns

4–6 sprigs of fresh thyme or 5 ml/1 tsp dried thyme

1 small bunch of coriander (6–8 sprigs), leaves and stems separated

For the garnish

1 small carrot

1 small leek, halved lengthways

4–6 shiitake mushrooms, thinly sliced

soy sauce

2 spring onions, thinly sliced

watercress or finely shredded Chinese leaves

freshly ground black pepper

1 Put the duck carcass and legs or giblets, onion, carrots, parsnip, leek and garlic in a large, heavy saucepan or flameproof casserole. Add the ginger, peppercorns, thyme and coriander stems, cover with cold water and bring to the boil over a medium-high heat, skimming off any foam that rises to the surface.

2 Reduce the heat and simmer gently for 1½–2 hours, then strain through a muslin-lined sieve into a bowl, discarding the bones and vegetables. Cool the stock and chill for several hours or overnight. Skim off any congealed fat and blot the surface with kitchen paper to remove any traces of fat.

3 To make the garnish, cut the carrot and leek into 5 cm/2 in pieces. Cut each piece lengthways in thin slices, then stack and slice into thin julienne strips. Place in a large saucepan with the sliced mushrooms.

4 Pour over the stock and add a few dashes of soy sauce and some pepper. Bring to the boil over a medium-high heat, skimming any foam that rises to the surface. Adjust the seasoning. Stir in the spring onions and watercress or Chinese leaves. Ladle the consommé into warmed bowls and sprinkle with the coriander leaves before serving.

Pork and Pickled Mustard Greens Soup

This highly flavoured soup makes an interesting start to a meal.

Serves 4–6

225 g/8 oz pickled mustard leaves, soaked
50 g/2 oz cellophane noodles, soaked
15 ml/1 tbsp vegetable oil
4 garlic cloves, finely sliced
1 litre/1¾ pints/4 cups chicken stock
450 g/1 lb pork ribs, cut into large chunks
30 ml/2 tbsp fish sauce
a pinch of sugar
freshly ground black pepper
2 fresh chillies, seeded and finely sliced,
   to garnish

1 Cut the pickled mustard leaves into bite-size pieces. Taste to check the seasoning. If they are too salty, soak them for a little longer.

2 Drain the cellophane noodles, discarding the soaking water, and cut them into pieces about 5 cm/2 in long.

3 Heat the oil in a small frying pan, add the garlic and stir-fry until golden. Transfer to a bowl and set aside.

4 Put the stock in a saucepan, bring to the boil, then add the pork ribs and simmer gently for 10–15 minutes.

5 Add the pickled mustard leaves and cellophane noodles. Bring back to the boil. Season to taste with fish sauce, sugar and freshly ground black pepper.

6 Pour the soup into individual serving bowls. Garnish with the fried garlic and the chillies and serve hot.

RICH &
CREAMY SOUPS

~

V

Broccoli and Almond Soup

The creaminess of the toasted almonds combines perfectly with the slightly bitter taste of the broccoli.

INGREDIENTS

Serves 4–6

50 g/2 oz/¹/₂ cup ground almonds

675 g/1¹/₂ lb broccoli

900 ml/1¹/₂ pints/3³/₄ cups vegetable stock or water

300 ml/¹/₂ pint/1¹/₄ cups skimmed milk

salt and freshly ground black pepper

1 Preheat the oven to 180°C/ 350°F/ Gas 4. Spread the ground almonds evenly on a baking sheet and toast in the oven for about 10 minutes until golden. Reserve one quarter of the almonds and set aside to garnish the finished dish.

2 Cut the broccoli into small florets and steam for about 6–7 minutes until tender.

3 Place the remaining toasted almonds, broccoli, stock or water and milk in a blender and blend until smooth. Season with salt and pepper to taste.

4 Reheat the soup and serve sprinkled with the reserved toasted almonds.

Broccoli and Stilton Soup

*This is a really easy but rich soup –
choose something simple to follow,
such as plainly roasted or grilled
meat, poultry or fish.*

INGREDIENTS

Serves 4

350 g/12 oz broccoli
25 g/l oz/2 tbsp butter
1 onion, chopped
1 leek, white part only, chopped
1 small potato, cut into chunks
600 ml/1 pint/2½ cups hot chicken stock
300 ml/½ pint/1¼ cups milk
45 ml/3 tbsp double cream
115 g/4 oz Stilton cheese, rind removed,
  crumbled
salt and freshly ground black pepper

1 Break the broccoli into florets,
discarding any tough stems.
Set aside two small florets to
garnish the finished dish.

2 Melt the butter in a large pan
and cook the onion and leek
until soft but not coloured. Add
the broccoli and potato, then pour
in the stock. Cover and simmer for
15–20 minutes, until the vegetables
are tender.

3 Cool slightly then pour into a
blender or food processor and
purée until smooth. Strain the
mixture through a sieve back into
the rinsed pan.

4 Add the milk and double
cream to the pan. Season to
taste with salt and freshly ground
black pepper. Reheat gently. At the
last minute add the cheese, stirring
until it just melts. Do not boil.

5 Meanwhile, blanch the
reserved broccoli florets and
cut them vertically into thin slices.
Ladle the soup into warmed bowls
and garnish with the sliced
broccoli and a generous grinding
of black pepper.

Tomato and Blue Cheese Soup

The concentrated flavour of roasted tomatoes strikes a great balance with strong blue cheese.

INGREDIENTS

Serves 4

1.5 kg/3 lb ripe tomatoes, peeled, quartered and seeded

2 garlic cloves, minced

30 ml/2 tbsp vegetable oil or butter

1 leek, chopped

1 carrot, chopped

1.2 litres/2 pints/5 cups chicken stock

115 g/4 oz blue cheese, crumbled

45 ml/3 tbsp whipping cream

several large fresh basil leaves, or 1–2 fresh parsley sprigs, plus extra to garnish

175 g/6 oz bacon, cooked and crumbled, to garnish

salt and freshly ground black pepper

1 Preheat the oven to 200°C/400°F/Gas 6. Spread the tomatoes in a shallow ovenproof dish. Sprinkle with the garlic and some salt and pepper. Place in the oven and bake for 35 minutes.

2 Heat the oil or butter in a large saucepan. Add the leek and carrot and season lightly with salt and pepper. Cook over low heat, stirring often, for about 10 minutes until softened.

3 Stir in the stock and baked tomatoes. Bring to the boil, then lower the heat, cover and simmer for about 20 minutes.

4 Add the blue cheese, cream and basil or parsley. Transfer to a food processor or blender and process until smooth (work in batches if necessary). Taste and adjust the seasoning.

5 Reheat the soup, but do not boil. Serve garnished with bacon and a sprig of fresh herbs.

Cauliflower and Walnut Cream

Even though there's no cream added to this soup, the cauliflower gives it a delicious, rich, creamy texture.

Serves 4

1 medium cauliflower

1 medium onion, roughly chopped

450 ml/¾ pint/scant 2 cups chicken or
    vegetable stock

450 ml/¾ pint/scant 2 cups skimmed milk

45 ml/3 tbsp walnut pieces

salt and freshly ground black pepper

paprika and chopped walnuts, to garnish

1 Trim the cauliflower of outer leaves and break into small florets. Place the cauliflower, onion and stock in a large saucepan.

2 Bring to the boil, cover and simmer for about 15 minutes until soft. Add the milk and walnut pieces, then purée in a blender or food processor until smooth.

3 Season the soup to taste with salt and pepper, then reheat and bring to the boil. Serve sprinkled with a dusting of paprika and chopped walnuts.

VARIATION
〜

If you prefer, you can make this soup using broccoli instead of cauliflower.

Carrot and Coriander Soup

Use a good home-made stock for this soup – it adds a far greater depth of flavour than stock made from cubes.

INGREDIENTS

Serves 4

50 g/2 oz/4 tbsp butter

3 leeks, sliced

450 g/1 lb carrots, sliced

15 ml/1 tbsp ground coriander

1.2 litres/2 pints/5 cups chicken stock

150 ml/¼ pint/⅔ cup Greek-style yogurt

salt and freshly ground black pepper

30–45 ml/2–3 tbsp chopped fresh
    coriander, to garnish

3 Leave to cool slightly, then purée the soup in a blender until smooth. Return the soup to the pan and add 30 ml/2 tbsp of the yogurt, then taste the soup and adjust the seasoning. Reheat gently, but do not boil.

4 Ladle the soup into bowls and put a spoonful of the remaining yogurt in the centre of each. Scatter over the chopped coriander and serve immediately.

1 Melt the butter in a large pan. Add the leeks and carrots and stir well. Cover and cook for 10 minutes, until the vegetables are beginning to soften.

2 Stir in the ground coriander and cook for about 1 minute. Pour in the stock and add seasoning to taste. Bring to the boil, cover and simmer for about 20 minutes, until the leeks and carrots are tender.

Carrot Soup with Ginger

The zing of fresh ginger is an ideal complement to the sweetness of cooked carrots.

INGREDIENTS

Serves 6

25 g/1 oz/2 tbsp butter or margarine
1 onion, chopped
1 celery stick, chopped
1 medium potato, chopped
675 g/1½ lb carrots, chopped
10 ml/2 tsp minced fresh root ginger
1.2 litres/2 pints/5 cups chicken stock
105 ml/7 tbsp whipping cream
a good pinch of freshly grated nutmeg
salt and freshly ground black pepper

1 Combine the butter or margarine, onion and celery and cook for about 5 minutes until softened.

2 Stir in the potato, carrots, ginger and stock. Bring to the boil. Reduce the heat to low, cover and simmer for about 20 minutes.

3 Pour the soup into a food processor or blender and process until it is smooth. Alternatively, use a vegetable mill to purée the soup. Return the soup to the pan. Stir in the cream and nutmeg and add salt and pepper to taste. Reheat gently to serve.

Jerusalem Artichoke Soup

Topped with saffron cream, this soup is wonderful on a chilly day.

INGREDIENTS

Serves 4

50 g/2 oz/4 tbsp butter

1 onion, chopped

450 g/1 lb Jerusalem artichokes, peeled and cut into chunks

900 ml/1½ pints/3¾ cups chicken stock

150 ml/¼ pint/⅔ cup milk

150 ml/¼ pint/⅔ cup double cream

a good pinch of saffron powder

salt and freshly ground black pepper

snipped fresh chives, to garnish

1 Melt the butter in a large, heavy-based pan and cook the onion for 5–8 minutes until soft but not browned, stirring from time to time.

2 Add the Jeruslaem artichokes to the pan and stir until coated in the butter. Cover and cook gently for 10–15 minutes, being careful not to allow the artichokes to brown. Pour in the chicken stock and milk, then cover and simmer for 15 minutes. Cool slightly, then process in a blender or food processor until smooth.

3 Strain the soup back into the pan. Add half the cream, season to taste and reheat gently. Lightly whip the remaining cream and the saffron powder. Ladle the soup into warmed soup bowls and put a spoonful of saffron cream in the centre of each. Scatter the snipped chives over the top and serve at once.

Spiced Parsnip Soup

*This pale, creamy-textured soup
is given a special touch with an
aromatic, spiced garlic and
coriander garnish.*

INGREDIENTS

Serves 4–6

40 g/1½ oz/3 tbsp butter
1 onion, chopped
675 g/1½ lb parsnips, diced
5 ml/1 tsp ground coriander
2.5 ml/½ tsp ground cumin
2.5 ml/½ tsp ground turmeric
1.5 ml/¼ tsp chilli powder
1.2 litres/2 pints/5 cups chicken stock
150 ml/¼ pint/⅔ cup single cream
15 ml/1 tbsp sunflower oil
1 garlic clove, cut into julienne strips
10 ml/2 tsp yellow mustard seeds
salt and freshly ground black pepper

1 Melt the butter in a large pan,
add the onion and parsnips
and fry gently for about 3 minutes.

2 Stir in the spices and cook for
1 minute more. Add the stock,
season with salt and pepper and
bring to the boil.

3 Reduce the heat, cover and
simmer for about 45 minutes,
until the parsnips are tender. Cool
slightly, then purée in a blender or
food processor until smooth.
Return the soup to the pan, add
the cream and heat through gently
over a low heat.

4 Heat the oil in a small pan,
add the julienne strips of
garlic and the yellow mustard
seeds and fry quickly until the
garlic is beginning to brown and
the mustard seeds start to pop and
splutter. Remove from the heat.

5 Ladle the soup into warmed
soup bowls and pour a little of
the hot spice mixture over each
one. Serve immediately.

Moroccan Vegetable Soup

Creamy parsnip and pumpkin give this soup a wonderfully rich texture.

INGREDIENTS

Serves 4

15 ml/1 tbsp olive or sunflower oil
15 g/½ oz/1 tbsp butter
1 onion, chopped
225 g/8 oz carrots, chopped
225 g/8 oz parsnips, chopped
225 g/8 oz pumpkin
about 900 ml/1½ pints/3¾ cups vegetable
    or chicken stock
lemon juice, to taste
salt and freshly ground black pepper

For the garnish
7.5 ml/1½ tsp olive oil
½ garlic clove, finely chopped
45 ml/3 tbsp chopped fresh parsley and
    coriander, mixed
a good pinch of paprika

1 Heat the oil and butter in a large pan and fry the onion for about 3 minutes until softened, stirring occasionally. Add the carrots and parsnips, stir well, cover and cook over a gentle heat for a further 5 minutes.

2 Cut the pumpkin into chunks, discarding the skin and pith, and stir into the pan. Cover and cook for a further 5 minutes, then add the stock and seasoning and slowly bring to the boil. Cover and simmer for 35–40 minutes until the vegetables are tender.

3 Allow the soup to cool slightly, then pour in to a food processor or blender and purée until smooth, adding a little extra water if the soup seems too thick. Pour back into a clean pan and reheat gently.

4 To make the garnish, heat the oil in a small pan and fry the garlic and herbs for 1–2 minutes. Add the paprika and stir well.

5 Adjust the seasoning of the soup and stir in lemon juice to taste. Pour into bowls and spoon a little of the prepared garnish on top, which should then be swirled carefully into the soup.

Creamy Courgette and Dolcelatte Soup

V

The beauty of this soup is its delicate colour, its creamy texture and its subtle taste. If you prefer a more pronounced cheese flavour, use Gorgonzola instead of Dolcelatte.

INGREDIENTS

Serves 4–6

30 ml/2 tbsp olive oil

15 g/½ oz/1 tbsp butter

1 medium onion, roughly chopped

900 g/2 lb courgettes, trimmed and sliced

5 ml/1 tsp dried oregano

about 600 ml/1 pint/2½ cups vegetable stock

115 g/4 oz Dolcelatte cheese, rind removed, diced

300 ml/½ pint/1¼ cups single cream

salt and freshly ground black pepper

To garnish

sprigs of fresh oregano

extra Dolcelatte cheese

1 Heat the oil and butter in a large saucepan until foaming. Add the onion and cook gently for about 5 minutes, stirring frequently, until softened but not brown.

2 Add the courgettes and oregano, with salt and pepper to taste. Cook over a medium heat for 10 minutes, stirring frequently.

3 Pour in the stock and bring to the boil, stirring frequently. Lower the heat, half-cover the pan and simmer gently, stirring occasionally, for about 30 minutes. Stir in the diced Dolcelatte until it is melted.

4 Process the soup in a blender or food processor until smooth, then press through a sieve into a clean pan.

5 Add two-thirds of the cream and stir over a low heat until hot, but not boiling. Check the consistency and add more stock if the soup is too thick. Taste and adjust seasoning if necessary.

6 Pour into heated bowls. Swirl in the remaining cream, garnish with fresh oregano and extra Dolcelatte cheese, crumbled, and serve.

Fresh Pea Soup St Germain

This soup takes its name from a suburb of Paris where peas used to be cultivated in market gardens.

INGREDIENTS

Serves 2–3

a small knob of butter

2 or 3 shallots, finely chopped

400 g/14 oz/3 cups shelled fresh peas
  (from about 1.5 kg/3 lb garden peas)

500 ml/17 fl oz/2¼ cups water

45–60 ml/3–4 tbsp whipping cream
  (optional)

salt and freshly ground black pepper

croûtons, to garnish

3 When the peas are tender, ladle them into a food processor or blender with a little of the cooking liquid and process until smooth.

4 Strain the soup into the saucepan or casserole, stir in the cream, if using, and heat through without boiling. Add the seasoning and serve hot, garnished with croûtons.

COOK'S TIP

If fresh peas are not available, use frozen peas, but thaw and rinse them before use.

1 Melt the butter in a heavy saucepan or flameproof casserole. Add the shallots and cook for about 3 minutes, stirring them occasionally.

2 Add the peas and water and season with salt and a little pepper. Cover and simmer for about 12 minutes for young peas and up to 18 minutes for large or older peas, stirring occasionally.

Green Bean and Parmesan Soup

V

Fresh green beans and Parmesan cheese make a simple but delicious combination of flavours.

INGREDIENTS

Serves 4

25 g/1 oz/2 tbsp butter or margarine

225 g/8 oz green beans, trimmed

1 garlic clove, crushed

450 ml/³⁄₄ pint/scant 2 cups vegetable stock

40 g/1¹⁄₂ oz/¹⁄₂ cup grated Parmesan cheese

50 ml/2 fl oz/¹⁄₄ cup single cream

salt and freshly ground black pepper

30 ml/2 tbsp chopped fresh parsley, to garnish

1 Melt the butter or margarine in a medium saucepan. Add the green beans and garlic and cook for 2–3 minutes over a medium heat, stirring frequently.

2 Stir in the stock and season with salt and pepper. Bring to the boil, then simmer, uncovered, for 10–15 minutes until the beans are tender.

3 Pour the soup into a blender or food processor and process until smooth. Alternatively, purée the soup in a food mill. Return to the pan and re-heat gently.

4 Stir in the Parmesan and cream. Sprinkle with the parsley and serve.

Cream of Spinach Soup

This is a deliciously creamy soup that you will find yourself making over and over again.

INGREDIENTS

Serves 4

25 g/1 oz/2 tbsp butter

1 small onion, chopped

675 g/1¹/₂ lb fresh spinach, chopped

1.2 litres/2 pints/5 cups vegetable stock

50 g/2 oz creamed coconut

freshly grated nutmeg

300 ml/¹/₂ pint/1¹/₄ cups single cream

salt and freshly ground black pepper

fresh snipped chives, to garnish

3 Return the mixture to the pan and add the remaining stock and the creamed coconut, with salt, pepper and nutmeg to taste. Simmer for 15 minutes to thicken.

4 Add the cream to the pan, stir well and heat through, but do not boil. Serve hot, garnished with long strips of chives.

1 Melt the butter in a saucepan over a moderate heat and sauté the onion for a few minutes until soft. Add the spinach, cover the pan and cook gently for 10 minutes, until the spinach has wilted and reduced.

2 Pour the spinach mixture into a blender or food processor and add a little of the stock. Blend until smooth.

Watercress Soup

V

*A delicious and nutritious soup
which should be served with
crusty bread.*

INGREDIENTS

Serves 4

15 ml/1 tbsp sunflower oil
15 g/¹/₂ oz/1 tbsp butter
1 medium onion, finely chopped
1 medium potato, diced
about 175 g/6 oz watercress
400 ml/14 fl oz/1²/₃ cups vegetable stock
400 ml/14 fl oz/1²/₃ cups milk
lemon juice, to taste
salt and freshly ground black pepper
soured cream, to serve

1 Heat the oil and butter in a
large saucepan and fry the
onion over a gentle heat until soft
but not browned. Add the potato,
fry gently for 2–3 minutes and
then cover and sweat for 5 minutes
over a gentle heat, stirring from
time to time.

2 Strip the watercress leaves
from the stalks and roughly
chop the stalks.

COOK'S TIP

Provided you leave out
the soured cream, this is
a low-calorie soup.

3 Add the stock and milk to the
pan, stir in the chopped stalks
and season. Bring to the boil and
simmer gently, partially covered,
for 10–12 minutes until the
potatoes are tender. Add all but
a few of the watercress leaves and
simmer for 2 minutes more.

4 Process the soup in a food
processor or blender and then
pour into a clean saucepan and
heat gently with the reserved
watercress leaves.

5 Taste the soup when hot, add
a little lemon juice and adjust
the seasoning.

6 Pour the soup into warmed
soup bowls and garnish with
a little soured cream in the centre
just before serving.

Cream of Avocado Soup

*Avocados make wonderful soup –
pretty, delicious and refreshing.*

INGREDIENTS

Serves 4

2 large ripe avocados
1 litre/1¾ pints/4 cups chicken stock
250 ml/8 fl oz/1 cup single cream
salt and freshly ground white pepper
15 ml/1 tbsp finely chopped fresh
    coriander, to garnish (optional)

1 Cut the avocados in half,
remove the stones and mash
the flesh. Put the flesh into a sieve
and press it through the sieve
with a wooden spoon into a warm
soup bowl.

2 Heat the chicken stock with
the cream in a saucepan.
When the mixture is hot, but not
boiling, whisk it into the puréed
avocado in the bowl.

3 Season to taste with salt and
pepper. Serve immediately,
sprinkled with the coriander, if
using. The soup may be served
chilled, if preferred.

Cream of Red Pepper Soup

*Grilling peppers gives them a sweet,
smoky flavour, which is delicious in
salads or, as here, in a velvety soup
with a secret flavouring of rosemary
to add aromatic depth. The soup is
equally good served hot or chilled,
as you prefer.*

INGREDIENTS

Serves 4

4 red peppers

25 g/1 oz/2 tbsp butter

1 onion, finely chopped

1 sprig of fresh rosemary

1.2 litres/2 pints/5 cups chicken or light
   vegetable stock

45 ml/3 tbsp tomato purée

120 ml/4 fl oz/½ cup double cream

paprika

salt and freshly ground black pepper

1 Preheat the grill. Put the
peppers in the grill pan under
the grill and turn them regularly
until the skins have blackened all
round. Put them into polythene
bags, sealing them closed. Leave
them for 20 minutes.

2 Peel the blackened skin off the
peppers. If possible avoid
rinsing them under the tap as this
loses some of the natural oil and
hence the flavour.

3 Halve the peppers, removing
the seeds, stalks and pith, then
roughly chop the flesh.

4 Melt the butter in a deep
saucepan. Add the onion and
rosemary and cook gently over a
low heat for about 5 minutes.
Remove the rosemary and discard.

5 Add the peppers and stock to
the onion, bring to the boil
and simmer for 15 minutes. Stir in
the tomato purée, then process or
sieve the soup to a smooth purée.

6 Stir in half the cream and
season with paprika, salt, if
necessary, and pepper.

7 Serve the soup hot or chilled,
with the remaining cream
swirled delicately on top. Speckle
the cream very lightly with a pinch
of paprika.

Creamy Tomato Soup

Tomato soup is an old favourite. This version is made special by the addition of fresh herbs and cream.

INGREDIENTS

Serves 4

25 g/1 oz/2 tbsp butter or margarine

1 onion, chopped

900 g/2 lb tomatoes, peeled and quartered

2 carrots, chopped

450 ml/³/₄ pint/scant 2 cups chicken stock

30 ml/2 tbsp chopped fresh parsley

2.5 ml/¹/₂ tsp fresh thyme leaves, plus
   extra to garnish

75 ml/5 tbsp whipping cream (optional)

salt and freshly ground black pepper

1 Melt the butter or margarine in a large saucepan. Add the onion and cook for 5 minutes until softened.

2 Stir in the tomatoes, carrots, chicken stock, parsley and thyme. Bring to the boil. Reduce the heat to low, cover the pan, and simmer for 15–20 minutes until the vegetables are tender.

3 Purée the soup in a vegetable mill until it is smooth. Return the puréed soup to the saucepan.

4 Stir in the cream, if using, and reheat gently. Season the soup to taste with salt and freshly ground black pepper. Ladle into warmed soup bowls and serve piping hot, garnished with fresh thyme leaves.

COOK'S TIP

Meaty and flavourful, Italian plum tomatoes are the best choice for this soup.

Cream of Spring Onion Soup

The oniony flavour of this soup is surprisingly delicate.

INGREDIENTS

Serves 4–6

25 g/1 oz/2 tbsp butter

1 small onion, chopped

150 g/5 oz/1¾ cups spring onions, chopped

225 g/8 oz potatoes, peeled and chopped

600 ml/1 pint/2½ cups vegetable stock

350 ml/12 fl oz/1½ cups single cream

30 ml/2 tbsp lemon juice

salt and freshly ground white pepper

chopped spring onion greens or fresh chives, to garnish

1 Melt the butter in a saucepan and add all the onions. Cover and cook over very low heat for about 10 minutes or until soft.

2 Add the potatoes and the stock. Bring to the boil, then cover again and simmer over moderately low heat for about 30 minutes. Cool slightly.

3 Purée the soup in a blender or food processor.

4 If serving the soup hot, pour it back into the pan. Add the cream and season with salt and pepper. Reheat gently, stirring occasionally. Add the lemon juice.

5 If serving the soup cold, pour it into a bowl. Stir in the cream and lemon juice and season with salt and pepper. Cover the bowl and chill for at least 1 hour.

6 Sprinkle with the chopped spring onion greens or chives before serving.

V

Cream of Celeriac and Spinach Soup

*Celeriac has a wonderful flavour
that is reminiscent of celery, but also
adds a slightly nutty taste. Here it is
combined with spinach to make a
delicious soup.*

INGREDIENTS

Serves 6

1 litre/1³⁄₄ pints/4 cups water
250 ml/8 fl oz/1 cup dry white wine
1 leek, thickly sliced
500 g/1¼ lb celeriac, diced
200 g/7 oz fresh spinach leaves
freshly grated nutmeg
salt and freshly ground black pepper
25 g/1 oz/¼ cup pine nuts, to garnish

1 Mix the water and wine in a
jug. Place the leek, celeriac and
spinach in a deep saucepan and
pour the liquid over the top. Bring
to the boil, lower the heat and
simmer for 10–15 minutes until
the vegetables are soft.

2 Pour the celeriac mixture into
a blender or food processor
and purée until smooth, in batches
if necessary. Return to the clean
pan and season to taste with salt,
ground black pepper and nutmeg.
Reheat gently.

3 Heat a non-stick frying pan
(do not add any oil) and add
the pine nuts. Roast until golden
brown, stirring occasionally so that
they do not stick. Sprinkle them
over the soup and serve.

C O O K ' S   T I P

If the soup is too thick, thin with
a little water or semi-skimmed
milk when puréeing.

Fresh Mushroom Soup with Tarragon

*This is a light mushroom soup,
subtly flavoured with tarragon.*

INGREDIENTS

Serves 6

15 g/¹⁄₂ oz/1 tbsp butter or margarine

4 shallots, finely chopped

450 g/1 1b/6 cups chestnut mushrooms,
  finely chopped

300 ml/¹⁄₂ pint/1¹⁄₄ cups vegetable stock

300 ml/¹⁄₂ pint/ 1¹⁄₄ cups semi-skimmed
  milk

15–30 ml/1–2 tbsp chopped fresh tarragon

30 ml/2 tbsp dry sherry (optional)

salt and freshly ground black pepper

sprigs of fresh tarragon, to garnish

1 Melt the butter or margarine
in a large saucepan, add the
shallots and cook gently for
5 minutes, stirring occasionally.
Add the mushrooms and cook
gently for 3 minutes, stirring. Add
the stock and milk.

2 Bring to the boil, then cover
and simmer gently for about
20 minutes until the vegetables
are soft. Stir in the chopped
tarragon and season to taste with
salt and pepper.

3 Allow the soup to cool slightly,
then purée in a blender or
food processor, in batches if
necessary, until smooth. Return to
the rinsed-out saucepan and
reheat gently.

4 Stir in the sherry, if using,
then ladle the soup into
warmed soup bowls and serve
garnished with sprigs of tarragon.

V A R I A T I O N

If you prefer, use a mixture of
wild and button mushrooms
rather than chestnut.

V

Cream of Mushroom Soup

A good mushroom soup makes the most of the subtle and sometimes rather elusive flavour of mushrooms. Button mushrooms are used here for their pale colour; chestnut or, better still, field mushrooms give a fuller flavour but turn the soup brown.

INGREDIENTS

Serves 4

275 g/10 oz button mushrooms
15 ml/1 tbsp sunflower oil
40 g/1½ oz/3 tbsp butter
1 small onion, finely chopped
15 ml/1 tbsp plain flour
450 ml/¾ pint/scant 2 cups vegetable stock
450 ml/¾ pint/scant 2 cups milk
a pinch of dried basil
30–45 ml/2–3 tbsp single cream (optional)
salt and freshly ground black pepper
fresh basil leaves, to garnish

1 Separate the mushroom caps from the stalks. Finely slice the caps and finely chop the stalks.

2 Heat the oil and half the butter in a heavy-based saucepan and add the onion, mushroom stalks and about three-quarters of the sliced mushroom caps. Fry for about 1–2 minutes, stirring frequently, then cover and sweat over a gentle heat for 6–7 minutes, stirring from time to time.

3 Stir in the flour and cook for about 1 minute. Gradually add the stock and milk, to make a smooth, thin sauce. Add the dried basil, and season to taste. Bring to the boil and simmer, partly covered, for 15 minutes.

4 Cool the soup slightly and then pour into a food processor or blender and process until smooth. Melt the rest of the butter in a frying pan and fry the remaining mushroom caps gently for 3–4 minutes until they are just tender.

5 Pour the soup into a clean saucepan and stir in the fried mushrooms. Heat until very hot and adjust the seasoning. Add the cream, if using. Serve sprinkled with fresh basil leaves.

Balinese Vegetable Soup

*Any seasonal vegetables can be used
in this soup, which is known as
Sayur Oelih.*

INGREDIENTS

Serves 8

225 g/8 oz green beans
1.2 litres/2 pints/5 cups boiling water
400 ml/14fl oz/1²/₃ cups coconut milk
1 garlic clove
2 macadamia nuts or 4 almonds
1 cm/½ in cube terasi
10–15 ml/2–3 tsp coriander seeds,
　dry-fried and ground
oil for frying
1 onion, finely sliced
2 duan salam or bay leaves
225 g/8 oz beansprouts
30 ml/2 tbsp lemon juice
salt

1 Top and tail the green beans
and cut into small pieces.
Cook the beans in the salted,
boiling water for 3–4 minutes.
Drain the beans and reserve the
cooking water.

2 Spoon off 45–60 ml/3–4 tbsp
of the cream from the top of
the coconut milk and set aside.

3 Grind the garlic, nuts, terasi
and ground coriander to a
paste in a food processor or with a
pestle and mortar.

4 Heat the oil in a wok or
saucepan and fry the onion
until transparent. Remove from
the pan and reserve. Fry the paste
for 2 minutes without browning.
Pour in the reserved bean cooking
water and coconut milk. Bring to
the boil and add the duan salam or
bay leaves. Cook, uncovered, for
15–20 minutes.

5 Just before serving, add the
beans, fried onion,
beansprouts, reserved coconut
cream and lemon juice. Taste and
adjust the seasoning, if necessary.
Serve at once.

V

Yogurt Soup

Some communities in India add sugar to this soup.

INGREDIENTS

Serves 4–6

450 ml/³⁄₄ pint/scant 2 cups natural yogurt, beaten

25 g/1 oz/¹⁄₄ cup gram flour (besan)

2.5 ml/¹⁄₂ tsp chilli powder

2.5 ml/¹⁄₂ tsp turmeric salt, to taste

2–3 fresh green chillies, finely chopped

60 ml/4 tbsp vegetable oil

1 whole dried red chilli

5 ml/1 tsp cumin seeds

3–4 curry leaves

3 garlic cloves, crushed

5 cm/2 in piece fresh root ginger, peeled and crushed

30 ml/2 tbsp chopped fresh coriander

1 Mix together the yogurt, flour, chilli powder and turmeric salt and pass through a strainer into a saucepan. Add the green chillies and cook gently for about 10 minutes, stirring occasionally. Be careful not to let the soup boil over.

2 Heat the oil in a frying pan and fry the remaining spices with the garlic and ginger until the dried chilli turns black. Stir in 15 ml/1 tbsp of the chopped fresh coriander.

3 Pour the spices over the yogurt soup, cover the pan and leave to rest for 5 minutes. Mix well and gently reheat for 5 minutes more. Serve hot, garnished with the remaining chopped coriander.

Egg and Cheese Soup

In this classic Roman soup, eggs and cheese are beaten into hot broth, producing a slightly "curdled" texture, which is a characteristic of the dish.

INGREDIENTS

Serves 6

3 eggs
45 ml/3 tbsp fine semolina
90 ml/6 tbsp grated Parmesan cheese
a pinch of freshly grated nutmeg
1.5 litres/2½ pints/6¼ cups meat or
   chicken stock
salt and freshly ground black pepper
12 slices French bread, to serve

1 Beat the eggs in a bowl with the semolina and cheese. Add the nutmeg. Beat in 250 ml/8 fl oz/ 1 cup of the cool stock.

2 Meanwhile, heat the leftover stock to simmering point in a large saucepan.

3 When the stock is hot, whisk the egg mixture into the stock. Raise the heat slightly and bring it barely to the boil. Season with salt and pepper. Cook for 3–4 minutes. As the egg cooks, the soup will lose its smooth consistency.

4 To serve, toast the slices of French bread and place 2 of them in the bottom of each soup plate. Ladle the hot soup on top of the bread and serve immediately.

Creamy Sweetcorn Soup

This is simple to prepare yet full of
flavour. It is sometimes made with
soured cream and cream cheese.
Poblano chillies may be added, but
these are rather difficult to locate
outside Mexico.

INGREDIENTS

Serves 4

30 ml/2 tbsp corn oil

1 onion, finely chopped

1 red pepper, seeded and chopped

450 g/1 lb/2²/₃ cups sweetcorn kernels,
  thawed if frozen

750 ml/1¼ pints/3 cups chicken stock

250 ml/8 fl oz/1 cup single cream

salt and freshly ground black pepper

½ red pepper, seeded and finely diced,
  to garnish

1 Heat the oil in a frying pan
and sauté the onion and red
pepper for about 5 minutes, until
soft. Add the sweetcorn and sauté
for 2 minutes.

2 Carefully tip the contents of
the pan into a food processor
or blender. Process until smooth,
scraping down the sides of the
blender and adding a little of the
stock, if necessary.

3 Transfer the mixture to a
saucepan and stir in the stock.
Season to taste with salt and
pepper, bring to a simmer and
cook for 5 minutes.

4 Gently stir in the cream. Serve
the soup hot or chilled,
sprinkled with the diced red
pepper. If serving hot, reheat
gently after adding the cream, but
do not allow the soup to boil.

White Bean Soup

Use either haricot beans or butter beans for this velvety soup.

INGREDIENTS

Serves 4

175 g/6 oz/³⁄₄ cup dried white beans,
    soaked in cold water overnight
30–45 ml/2–3 tbsp oil
2 large onions, chopped
4 celery sticks, chopped
1 parsnip, chopped
1 litre/1³⁄₄ pints/4 cups chicken stock
salt and freshly ground black pepper
chopped fresh coriander and paprika,
    to garnish

1 Drain the beans and boil rapidly in fresh water for 10 minutes. Drain, cover with more fresh water and simmer for 1–2 hours until soft. Reserve the liquid and discard any bean skins on the surface.

2 Heat the oil in a heavy pan and sauté the onions, celery and parsnip for 3 minutes.

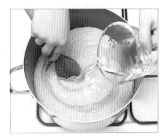

COOK'S TIP
～

You can, if you prefer, use a 400 g/14 oz can cannellini or butter beans instead of dried beans. Drain and rinse them before adding to the dish.

---

3 Add the cooked beans and stock and continue cooking until the vegetables are tender. Allow the soup to cool slightly and, using a food processor or hand blender, blend the soup until it is velvety smooth.

4 Reheat the soup gently, gradually adding some of the bean liquid or a little water if it is too thick. Season to taste.

5 To serve, transfer the soup into wide bowls. Garnish with fresh coriander and paprika.

Pumpkin and Coconut Soup

Rich and sweet flavours are married beautifully with sharp and hot in this creamy South-east Asian-influenced soup.

INGREDIENTS

Serves 4–6

2 garlic cloves, crushed
4 shallots, finely crushed
2.5 ml/½ tsp shrimp paste
15 ml/1 tbsp dried shrimps, soaked
    for 10 minutes and drained
1 lemon grass stalk, chopped
2 fresh green chillies, seeded
600 ml/1 pint/2½ cups chicken stock
450 g/1 lb pumpkin, cut into 2 cm/¾ in
    thick chunks
600 ml/1 pint/2½ cups coconut cream
30 ml/2 tbsp fish sauce
5 ml/1 tsp sugar
115 g/4 oz small cooked peeled prawns
salt and freshly ground black pepper
to garnish:
    2 fresh red chillies, seeded and finely
        sliced
    10–12 fresh basil leaves

5 Add the prawns and cook until they are heated through. Serve garnished with the sliced red chillies and basil leaves.

1 Using a pestle and mortar, grind the garlic, shallots, shrimp paste, dried shrimps, lemon grass, green chillies and a pinch of salt into a paste.

2 In a large saucepan, bring the chicken stock to the boil, add the paste and stir until dissolved.

3 Lower the heat, add the pumpkin, and simmer for about 10–15 minutes or until the pumpkin is tender.

4 Stir in the coconut cream, then bring back to a simmer. Add the fish sauce, sugar and ground black pepper to taste.

COOK'S TIP

Shrimp paste, which is made from ground shrimps fermented in brine, is used to give food a savoury flavour.

Shrimp and Corn Bisque

*Hot pepper sauce brings a touch of
spice to this mild, creamy soup.*

INGREDIENTS

Serves 4

30 ml/2 tbsp olive oil
1 onion, finely minced
50 g/2 oz/4 tbsp butter or margarine
25 g/1 oz/¼ cup flour
750 ml/1¼ pints/3 cups fish stock
250 ml/8 fl oz/1 cup milk
115 g/4 oz/1 cup peeled cooked small
    shrimps, deveined if necessary
225 g/8 oz/1½ cups sweetcorn kernels
2.5 ml/½ tsp chopped fresh dill or thyme
hot pepper sauce
120 ml/4 fl oz/½ cup single cream
salt
sprigs of fresh dill, to garnish

1 Heat the olive oil in a large
heavy saucepan. Add the
onion and cook over a low heat for
8–10 minutes until softened.

2 Meanwhile, melt the butter or
margarine in a medium-sized
saucepan. Add the flour and cook
for 1–2 minutes, stirring. Stir in
the stock and milk, bring to the
boil and cook for 5–8 minutes,
stirring frequently.

3 Cut each shrimp into two or
three pieces and add to the
onion with the corn and dill or
thyme. Cook for 2–3 minutes,
then remove from the heat.

4 Add the sauce mixture to the
shrimp and corn mixture, and
mix well. Remove 750 ml/1¼ pints/
3 cups of the soup and purée in a
blender or food processor. Return
it to the rest of the soup in the pan
and stir well. Season with salt and
hot pepper sauce to taste.

5 Add the cream and stir to
blend. Heat the soup almost to
boiling point, stirring frequently.

6 Divide into individual soup
bowls and serve hot, garnished
with sprigs of dill.

Prawn Bisque

The classic French method for making a bisque requires pushing the shellfish through a tamis, or drum sieve. This recipe is simpler and the result is just as smooth.

INGREDIENTS

Serves 6-8

675 g/1½ lb small or medium cooked
  prawns in their shells
25 ml/1½ tbsp vegetable oil
2 onions, halved and sliced
1 large carrot, sliced
2 celery sticks, sliced
2 litres/3½ pints/9 cups water
a few drops of lemon juice
30 ml/2 tbsp tomato purée
bouquet garni
50 g/2 oz/4 tbsp butter
50 g/2 oz/⅓ cup plain flour
45-60 ml/3-4 tbsp brandy
150 ml/¼ pint/⅔ cup whipping cream

1 Remove the heads from the prawns and peel away the shells. Reserve the heads and shells for the stock. Place the prawns in a covered bowl in the refrigerator.

2 Heat the oil in a large saucepan, add the heads and shells and cook over a high heat, stirring, until they start to brown. Reduce the heat to medium, add the vegetables and fry, stirring occasionally, for 5 minutes until the onions soften.

3 Add the water, lemon juice, tomato purée and bouquet garni. Bring the stock to the boil, then reduce the heat, cover and simmer gently for 25 minutes. Strain the stock through a sieve.

4 Melt the butter in a heavy saucepan over a medium heat. Stir in the flour and cook until just golden, stirring occasionally.

5 Add the brandy. Gradually pour in half the prawn stock, whisking vigorously until smooth, then whisk in the remaining liquid. Season if necessary. Reduce the heat, cover and simmer for 5 minutes, stirring frequently.

6 Strain the soup into a clean saucepan. Add the cream and a little extra lemon juice to taste, then stir in most of the reserved prawns and cook over a medium heat, stirring frequently, until hot. Serve at once, garnished with the remaining reserved prawns.

COOK'S TIP

If you prefer you may leave the brandy out of this dish and it will still taste delicious.

Fish and Sweet Potato Soup

The subtle sweetness of the potato, combined with the fish and the aromatic flavour of oregano, makes this an appetizing soup.

INGREDIENTS

Serves 4

¹/₂ onion, chopped

175 g/6 oz sweet potato, peeled and diced

175 g/6 oz boneless white fish fillet, skinned

50 g/2 oz carrot, chopped

5 ml/1 tsp chopped fresh oregano or 2.5 ml/¹/₂ tsp dried oregano

2.5 ml/¹/₂ tsp ground cinnamon

1.5 litres/2¹/₂ pints/6¹/₄ cups fish stock

75 ml/5 tbsp single cream

chopped fresh parsley, to garnish

1 Put the chopped onion, diced sweet potato, white fish, chopped carrot, oregano, cinnamon and half of the fish stock in a saucepan. Bring to the boil, then simmer for 20 minutes or until the potato is cooked.

2 Allow to cool, then pour into a blender or food processor and blend until smooth.

3 Return the soup to the saucepan, then add the remaining fish stock and gently bring to the boil. Reduce the heat to low and add the single cream, then gently heat through without boiling, stirring occasionally.

4 Serve hot in warmed soup bowls, garnished with the chopped fresh parsley.

VARIATION
~
Garnish with chopped fresh tarragon instead of parsley.

Squash Soup with Horseradish Cream

V

The combination of cream, curry powder and horseradish makes a wonderful topping for this beautiful golden soup.

INGREDIENTS

Serves 6

1 butternut squash
1 cooking apple
25 g/1 oz/2 tbsp butter
1 onion, finely chopped
5–10 ml/1–2 tsp curry powder, plus extra
    to garnish
900 ml/1½ pints/3¾ cups vegetable stock
5 ml/1 tsp chopped fresh sage
150 ml/¼ pint/⅔ cup apple juice
salt and freshly ground black pepper
lime shreds, to garnish (optional)

For the horseradish cream
60 ml/4 tbsp double cream
10 ml/2 tsp horseradish sauce
2.5 ml/½ tsp curry powder

1 Peel the squash, remove the seeds and chop the flesh. Peel, core and chop the apple.

2 Heat the butter in a large saucepan. Add the onion and cook, stirring occasionally, for 5 minutes until soft. Stir in the curry powder. Cook to bring out the flavour, stirring constantly, for 2 minutes.

3 Add the stock, squash, apple and sage. Bring to the boil, lower the heat, cover and simmer for 20 minutes until the squash and apple are soft.

4 Meanwhile, make the horseradish cream. Whip the cream in a bowl until stiff, then stir in the horseradish sauce and curry powder. Cover and chill until required.

5 Purée the soup in a blender or food processor. Return to the clean pan and add the apple juice, with salt and pepper to taste. Reheat gently, without boiling.

6 Serve the soup in bowls, topped with a spoonful of horseradish cream and a dusting of curry powder. Garnish with a few lime shreds, if you like.

Thai-style Chicken Soup

A fragrant blend of coconut milk, lemon grass, ginger and lime makes a delicious soup, with just a hint of warming chilli.

INGREDIENTS

Serves 4

5 ml/1 tsp oil

1–2 fresh red chillies, seeded and chopped

2 garlic cloves, crushed

1 large leek, finely sliced

600 ml/1 pint/2½ cups chicken stock

400 ml/14 fl oz/1⅔ cups coconut milk

450 g/1 lb skinless boneless chicken
  thighs, cut into bite-size pieces

30 ml/2 tbsp Thai fish sauce

1 lemon grass stalk, split

2.5 cm/1 in piece fresh root ginger, peeled
  and finely chopped

5 ml/1 tsp sugar

4 kaffir lime leaves (optional)

75 g/3 oz/¾ cup frozen peas, thawed

45 ml/3 tbsp chopped fresh coriander

3 Add the chicken, fish sauce, lemon grass, ginger, sugar and lime leaves, if using. Lower the heat and simmer, covered, for 15 minutes until the chicken is tender, stirring occasionally.

4 Add the peas and cook for a further 3 minutes. Remove the lemon grass and stir in the coriander just before serving.

1 Heat the oil in a large saucepan and cook the chillies and garlic for about 2 minutes. Add the leek and cook for a further 2 minutes.

2 Stir in the stock and coconut milk and bring to the boil over a medium-high heat.

Spicy Chicken and Mushroom Soup

*This creamy chicken soup makes a
hearty meal. Serve it piping hot with
fresh garlic bread.*

INGREDIENTS

Serves 4

75 g/3 oz/6 tbsp unsalted butter

2.5 ml/½ tsp crushed garlic

5 ml/1 tsp garam masala

5 ml/1 tsp crushed black peppercorns

5 ml/1 tsp salt

1.5 ml/¼ tsp freshly grated nutmeg

225 g/8 oz chicken, skinned and boned

1 medium leek, sliced

75 g/3 oz/generous 1 cup mushrooms,
   sliced

50 g/2 oz/⅓ cup sweetcorn kernels

300 ml/½ pint/1¼ cups water

250 ml/8 fl oz/1 cup single cream

30 ml/2 tbsp chopped fresh coriander

5 ml/1 tsp crushed dried red chillies, to
   garnish (optional)

1 Melt the butter in a medium
saucepan. Lower the heat
slightly and add the garlic and
garam masala. Lower the heat even
further and add the black
peppercorns, salt and nutmeg.

2 Cut the chicken pieces into
very fine strips and add to the
pan with the leek, mushrooms and
sweetcorn. Cook for 5–7 minutes
until the chicken is cooked
through, stirring constantly.

3 Remove from the heat and
allow to cool slightly. Transfer
three-quarters of the mixture into
a food processor or blender. Add
the water and process for about
1 minute.

4 Pour the resulting purée back
into the saucepan with the rest
of the mixture and bring to the
boil over a medium heat. Lower
the heat and stir in the cream.

5 Add the fresh coriander. Taste
and adjust the seasoning.
Serve hot, garnished with crushed
red chillies, if liked.

Chicken and Almond Soup

This soup makes an excellent lunch or supper dish when served with naan bread.

INGREDIENTS

Serves 4

75 g/3 oz/6 tbsp unsalted butter
1 medium leek, chopped
2.5 ml/¹/₂ tsp shredded fresh root ginger
75 g/3 oz/³/₄ cup ground almonds
5 ml/1 tsp salt
2.5 ml/¹/₂ tsp crushed black peppercorns
1 fresh green chilli, chopped
1 medium carrot, sliced
50 g/2 oz/¹/₂ cup frozen peas
115 g/4 oz/1 cup chicken, skinned, boned
 and cubed
30 ml/2 tbsp chopped fresh coriander
450 ml/³/₄ pint/scant 2 cups water
250 ml/8 fl oz/1 cup single cream
4 sprigs of fresh coriander

1 Melt the unsalted butter in a deep, round-bottomed frying pan, and sauté the chopped leek and the root ginger until soft but only just turning brown.

2 Lower the heat and add the ground almonds, salt, peppercorns, chilli, carrot, peas and chicken. Fry for about 10 minutes or until the chicken is completely cooked, stirring constantly. Add the chopped fresh coriander.

3 Remove from the heat and allow to cool slightly. Transfer the mixture to a food processor or blender and process for about 1¹/₂ minutes. Pour in the water and blend for a further 30 seconds.

4 Pour back into the saucepan and bring to the boil, stirring occasionally. Once it has boiled, lower the heat and gradually stir in the cream. Cook gently for a further 2 minutes, stirring from time to time. Serve garnished with the sprigs of fresh coriander.

WINTER
WARMING SOUPS

~

V

Borscht

A simply stunning colour, this classic Russian soup is the perfect dish to serve when you want to offer something a little different.

INGREDIENTS

Serves 6

1 onion, chopped

450 g/1 lb raw beetroot, peeled and
  chopped

2 celery sticks, chopped

1/2 red pepper, chopped

115 g/4 oz mushrooms, chopped

1 large cooking apple, chopped

25 g/1 oz/2 tbsp butter

30 ml/2 tbsp sunflower oil

2 litres/3½ pints/9 cups stock or water

5 ml/1 tsp cumin seeds

a pinch of dried thyme

1 large bay leaf

fresh lemon juice

salt and freshly ground black pepper

For the garnish

150 ml/1/4 pint/2/3 cup soured cream

a few sprigs of fresh dill

1 Place the chopped vegetables and apple in a large saucepan with the butter, oil and 45 ml/3 tbsp of the stock or water. Cover and cook gently for about 15 minutes, shaking the pan occasionally.

2 Stir in the cumin seeds and cook for 1 minute, then add the remaining stock or water, the thyme, bay leaf, lemon juice and seasoning to taste.

3 Bring the mixture to the boil, then cover the pan and turn down the heat to a gentle simmer. Cook for about 30 minutes.

4 Strain the vegetables and reserve the liquid. Process the vegetables in a food processor or blender until they are smooth and creamy.

5 Return the vegetables to the pan, add the reserved stock and reheat. Check the seasoning.

6 Divide into individual serving bowls. Garnish with swirls of soured cream in each bowl and top with a few sprigs of fresh dill.

COOK'S TIP

The flavour of this marvellous soup matures and improves if it is made the day before it is needed.

V

Curried Celery Soup

An unusual but stimulating combination of flavours, this warming soup is an excellent way to transform celery. Serve with warm wholemeal bread rolls.

INGREDIENTS

Serves 4–6

10 ml/2 tsp olive oil

1 onion, chopped

1 leek, sliced

675 g/1½ lb celery, chopped

15 ml/1 tbsp medium or hot
   curry powder

225 g/8 oz unpeeled potatoes, washed
   and diced

900 ml/1½ pints/3¾ cups vegetable stock

1 bouquet garni

30 ml/2 tbsp chopped fresh mixed herbs

salt

celery seeds and leaves, to garnish

1 Heat the oil in a large saucepan. Add the onion, leek and celery, cover and cook gently for about 10 minutes, stirring occasionally.

2 Add the curry powder and cook gently for 2 minutes, stirring from time to time.

3 Add the potatoes, stock and bouquet garni, cover and bring to the boil. Simmer for about 20 minutes, until the vegetables are tender, but not too soft.

4 Remove and discard the bouquet garni and set the soup aside to cool slightly before it is processed.

5 Transfer the soup to a blender or food processor and process in batches until smooth.

6 Add the mixed herbs, season to taste with salt and process briefly again. Return to the saucepan and reheat gently until piping hot. Ladle into bowls and garnish each one with a sprinkling of celery seeds and a few celery leaves before serving.

VARIATION

For a change, use celeriac and sweet potatoes in place of celery and standard potatoes.

Nettle Soup

A country-style soup which is a tasty variation of the classic Irish potato soup. Use wild nettles if you can find them, or a washed head of round lettuce if you prefer.

INGREDIENTS

Serves 4

115 g/4 oz/½ cup butter
450 g/1 lb onions, sliced
450 g/1 lb potatoes, cut into chunks
750 ml/1¼ pints/3 cups chicken stock
25 g/1 oz nettle leaves
a small bunch of chives, snipped
salt and freshly ground black pepper
double cream, to serve

2 Wearing rubber gloves, remove the nettle leaves from their stalks. Wash the leaves under cold running water, then dry on kitchen paper. Add to the saucepan and cook for a further 5 minutes.

3 Ladle the soup into a blender or food processor and process until smooth. Return to a clean saucepan and season well. Stir in the chives and serve with a swirl of cream and a sprinkling of pepper.

1 Melt the butter in a large saucepan and add the sliced onions. Cover and cook for about 5 minutes until just softened. Add the potatoes to the saucepan with the chicken stock. Cover and cook for 25 minutes.

COOK'S TIP

If you prefer, cut the vegetables finely and leave the cooked soup chunky rather than puréeing it.

Leek, Parsnip and Ginger Soup

V

A flavoursome winter warmer, with the added spiciness of fresh ginger.

INGREDIENTS

Serves 4–6

30 ml/2 tbsp olive oil

225 g/8 oz/2 cups leeks, sliced

25 g/1 oz fresh root ginger, peeled and finely chopped

675 g/1½ lb/5 cups parsnips, roughly chopped

300 ml/½ pint/1¼ cups dry white wine

1.2 litres/2 pints/5 cups vegetable stock or water

salt and freshly ground black pepper

fromage blanc and paprika, to garnish

1 Heat the oil in a large pan and add the leeks and ginger. Cook gently for 2–3 minutes until the leeks start to soften.

2 Add the parsnips and cook for a further 7–8 minutes until they are beginning to soften.

3 Pour in the wine and stock or water and bring to the boil. Reduce the heat and simmer for 20–30 minutes or until the parsnips are tender.

4 Purée in a blender or food processor until smooth. Season to taste. Reheat and garnish with a swirl of fromage blanc and a light dusting of paprika.

Green Pea Soup with Spinach

This lovely green soup was invented by the wife of a 17th-century British Member of Parliament, and it has stood the test of time.

INGREDIENTS

Serves 6

450 g/1 lb/generous 3 cups podded fresh
   or frozen peas
1 leek, finely sliced
2 garlic cloves, crushed
2 rindless back bacon rashers, finely diced
1.2 litres/2 pints/5 cups ham or
   chicken stock
30 ml/2 tbsp olive oil
50 g/2 oz fresh spinach, shredded
40 g/1½ oz/⅓ cup white cabbage,
   finely shredded
½ small lettuce, finely shredded
1 celery stick, finely chopped
a large handful of parsley, finely chopped
½ carton mustard and cress
20 ml/4 tsp chopped fresh mint
a pinch of ground mace
salt and freshly ground black pepper

1 Put the peas, leek, garlic and bacon in a large saucepan. Add the stock, bring to the boil, then lower the heat and simmer for 20 minutes.

2 About 5 minutes before the pea mixture is ready, heat the oil in another large saucepan.

3 Add the spinach, cabbage, lettuce, celery and herbs to the frying pan. Cover and sweat the mixture over a low heat until soft.

4 Transfer the pea mixture to a blender or food processor and process until smooth. Add to the sweated vegetables and herbs and heat through. Season with mace, salt and pepper and serve.

Spicy Carrot Soup with Garlic Croûtons

V

Carrot soup is given a touch of spice with coriander, cumin and chilli powder.

INGREDIENTS

Serves 6

15 ml/l tbsp olive oil

1 large onion, chopped

675 g/1½ lb/3¾ cups carrots, sliced

5 ml/1 tsp each ground coriander, ground cumin and hot chilli powder

900 ml/1½ pints/3¾ cups vegetable stock

salt and freshly ground black pepper

sprigs of fresh coriander, to garnish

For the garlic croûtons

a little olive oil

2 garlic cloves, crushed

4 slices bread, crusts removed, cut into 1 cm/½ in cubes

1 To make the soup, heat the oil in a large saucepan, add the onion and carrots and cook gently for 5 minutes, stirring occasionally. Add the ground spices and cook gently for 1 minute, continuing to stir.

2 Stir in the stock, bring to the boil, then cover and cook gently for about 45 minutes until the carrots are tender.

3 Meanwhile, make the garlic croûtons. Heat the oil in a frying pan, add the garlic and cook gently for 30 seconds, stirring. Add the bread cubes, turn them over in the oil and fry over a medium heat for a few minutes until crisp and golden brown all over, turning frequently. Drain on kitchen paper and keep warm.

4 Purée the soup in a blender or food processor until smooth, then season to taste with salt and pepper. Return the soup to the rinsed-out saucepan and reheat gently. Serve hot, sprinkled with garlic croûtons and garnished with coriander sprigs.

Curried Carrot and Apple Soup

The combination of carrot, curry and apple is a highly successful one. Curried fruit is delicious.

INGREDIENTS

Serves 4

10 ml/2 tsp sunflower oil

15 ml/1 tbsp mild Korma curry powder

500 g/1¼ lb carrots, chopped

1 large onion, chopped

1 Bramley cooking apple, chopped

750 ml/1¼ pints/3 cups chicken stock

salt and freshly ground black pepper

natural yogurt and carrot curls, to garnish

1 Heat the oil in a large, heavy-based pan and gently fry the curry powder for 2–3 minutes.

2 Add the chopped carrots and onion and the cooking apple, stir well until coated with the curry powder, then cover the pan.

3 Cook over a low heat for about 15 minutes, shaking the pan occasionally, until softened. Spoon the vegetable mixture into a food processor or blender, then add half the stock and process until smooth.

4 Return to the pan and pour in the remaining stock. Bring the soup to the boil and adjust the seasoning before serving in bowls, garnished with a swirl of yogurt and a few curls of raw carrot.

Pumpkin Soup

*The sweet flavour of pumpkin is
excellent in soups, teaming well with
other savoury ingredients such as
onions and potatoes to make a
warm and comforting dish. For
added flavour, try roasting the
pumpkin chunks instead before
adding to the soup with the stock.*

INGREDIENTS

Serves 4–6

15 ml/1 tbsp sunflower oil

25 g/l oz/2 tbsp butter

1 large onion, sliced

675 g/1½ lb pumpkin, cut into
   large chunks

450 g/1 lb potatoes, sliced

600 ml/1 pint/2½ cups vegetable stock

a good pinch of freshly grated nutmeg

5 ml/1 tsp chopped fresh tarragon

600 ml/1 pint/2½ cups milk

about 5–10 ml/1–2 tsp lemon juice

salt and freshly ground black pepper

1 Heat the oil and butter in a
heavy-based saucepan and fry
the onion for 4–5 minutes over a
gentle heat until soft but not
browned, stirring frequently.

2 Add the pumpkin and sliced
potatoes, stir well, then cover
and sweat over a low heat for about
10 minutes until the vegetables are
almost tender, stirring occasionally
to stop them sticking to the pan.

3 Stir in the stock, nutmeg,
tarragon and seasoning. Bring
to the boil and then simmer for
about 10 minutes until the
vegetables are completely tender.

4 Allow to cool slightly, then
pour into a food processor or
blender and process until smooth.
Pour back into a clean saucepan
and add the milk. Heat gently and
then taste, adding the lemon juice
and extra seasoning, if necessary.
Serve piping hot.

Sweet Potato and Red Pepper Soup

V

As colourful as it is good to eat, this soup is a sure winner.

Serves 6

2 red peppers (about 225 g/8 oz) seeded
   and cubed

500 g/1¼ lb sweet potatoes, cubed

1 onion, roughly chopped

2 large garlic cloves, roughly chopped

300 ml/½ pint/1¼ cups dry white wine

1.2 litres/2 pints/5 cups vegetable
   stock

Tabasco sauce, to taste

salt and freshly ground black pepper

fresh country bread, to serve

1 Dice a small quantity of red pepper for the garnish and set aside. Put the rest into a saucepan with the sweet potato, onion, garlic, wine and vegetable stock. Bring to the boil, lower the heat and simmer for 30 minutes or until all the vegetables are quite soft.

2 Transfer the mixture to a blender or food processor and process until smooth. Season to taste with salt, pepper and a generous dash of Tabasco. Cool slightly. Garnish with the reserved diced red pepper and serve warm or at room temperature.

Sweet Potato and Parsnip Soup

The sweetness of the two root vegetables comes through strongly in this delicious soup.

INGREDIENTS

Serves 6

15 ml/1 tbsp sunflower oil

1 large leek, sliced

2 celery sticks, chopped

450 g/1 lb sweet potatoes, diced

225 g/8 oz/1½ cups parsnips, diced

900 ml/1½ pints/3¾ cups vegetable stock

salt and freshly ground black pepper

For the garnish

15 ml/1 tbsp chopped fresh parsley

roasted strips of sweet potatoes and parsnips

1 Heat the oil in a large saucepan and add the leek, celery, sweet potatoes and parsnips. Cook gently for about 5 minutes, stirring to prevent them browning or sticking to the pan.

2 Stir in the vegetable stock and bring to the boil, then cover and simmer gently for about 25 minutes, or until the vegetables are tender, stirring occasionally. Season to taste. Remove the pan from the heat and allow the soup to cool slightly.

3 Purée the soup in a blender or food processor until smooth, then return the soup to the pan and reheat gently. Ladle into warmed soup bowls to serve and sprinkle over the chopped parsley and roasted strips of sweet potatoes and parsnips.

Root Vegetable Soup

Simmer a selection of popular winter root vegetables together for a warming and satisfying soup. Its creamy taste comes from adding crème fraîche just before serving.

INGREDIENTS

Serves 6

3 medium carrots, chopped

1 large potato, chopped

1 large parsnip, chopped

1 large turnip or small swede, chopped

1 onion, chopped

30 ml/2 tbsp sunflower oil

25 g/1 oz/2 tbsp butter

1.5 litres/2½ pints/6¼ cups water

1 piece fresh root ginger, peeled and
    grated

300 ml/½ pint/1¼ cups milk

45 ml/3 tbsp crème fraîche or fromage
    frais

30 ml/2 tbsp chopped fresh dill

15 ml/1 tbsp lemon juice

salt and freshly ground black pepper

sprigs of fresh dill, to garnish

1 Put the carrots, potato, parsnip, turnip or swede and onion into a large saucepan with the oil and butter. Fry lightly, then cover and sweat the vegetables on a low heat for 15 minutes, shaking the pan occasionally.

2 Pour in the water, bring to the boil and season well. Cover and simmer for 20 minutes until the vegetables are soft.

3 Strain the vegetables, reserving the stock, add the ginger and vegetables to a food processor or blender and purée until smooth. Return the puréed mixture and stock to the pan. Add the milk and stir while the soup gently reheats.

4 Remove from the heat and stir in the crème fraîche or fromage frais, plus the dill and lemon juice. Season if necessary. Reheat the soup but do not allow it to boil or it may curdle. Serve garnished with sprigs of dill.

Leek and Thyme Soup

V

This is a filling, heart-warming soup, which can be liquidized to a smooth purée or served as it is here, in its original peasant style.

INGREDIENTS

Serves 4

900 g/2 lb leeks

450 g/1 lb potatoes

115 g/4 oz/^{1}/$_{2}$ cup butter

1 large sprig of fresh thyme, plus extra to garnish (optional)

300 ml/^{1}/$_{2}$ pint/1^{1}/$_{4}$ cups milk

salt and freshly ground black pepper

60 ml/4 tbsp double cream, to serve

1 Top and tail the leeks. If you are using big winter leeks, strip away all the coarse outer leaves, then cut the leeks into thick slices. Wash thoroughly under cold running water.

2 Cut the potatoes into rough dice, about 2.5 cm/1 in, and dry on kitchen paper.

3 Melt the butter in a large saucepan and add the leeks and 1 sprig of thyme. Cover and cook for 4–5 minutes until softened. Add the potato pieces and just enough cold water to cover the vegetables. Re-cover and cook over a low heat for 30 minutes.

4 Pour in the milk and season with salt and pepper. Cover and simmer for a further 30 minutes. You will find that some of the potato breaks up, leaving you with a semi-puréed and rather lumpy soup.

5 Remove the sprig of thyme (the leaves will have fallen into the soup) and serve, adding 15 ml/ 1 tbsp cream and a garnish of thyme to each portion, if using.

Mushroom and Herb Potage

Do not worry if this soup is not completely smooth – it is especially nice when it has a slightly nutty, textured consistency.

INGREDIENTS

Serves 4

50 g/2 oz smoked streaky bacon

1 onion, chopped

15 ml/1 tbsp sunflower oil

350 g/12 oz open field mushrooms or a
     mixture of wild and brown mushrooms

600 ml/1 pint/2½ cups good meat stock

30 ml/2 tbsp sweet sherry

30 ml/2 tbsp chopped fresh mixed herbs,
     such as sage, rosemary, thyme and
     marjoram, or 10 ml/2 tsp dried herbs

salt and freshly ground black pepper

a few sprigs of sage or marjoram,
     to garnish

60 ml/4 tbsp thick Greek-style yogurt or
     crème fraîche, to serve

1 Roughly chop the bacon and place in a large saucepan. Cook gently until all the fat comes out of the bacon.

2 Add the onion and soften, adding oil if necessary. Wipe the mushrooms clean, roughly chop and add to the pan. Cover and sweat until they have completely softened and their liquid has run out.

3 Add the stock, sherry, herbs and seasoning, cover and simmer for 10–12 minutes. Process the soup in a food processor or blender until smooth, but don't worry if you still have a slightly textured result.

4 Check the seasoning and heat through. Serve with a dollop of yogurt or crème fraîche and a sprig of fresh sage or marjoram in each bowl.

Mushroom, Celery and Garlic Soup

A robust soup in which the dominant flavour of mushrooms is enhanced with garlic, while celery introduces a contrasting note.

INGREDIENTS

Serves 4

350 g/12 oz/4½ cups chopped mushrooms

4 celery sticks, chopped

3 garlic cloves

45 ml/3 tbsp dry sherry or white wine

750 ml/1¼ pints/3 cups chicken stock

30 ml/2 tbsp Worcestershire sauce

5 ml/1 tsp freshly grated nutmeg

salt and freshly ground black pepper

celery leaves, to garnish

1 Place the mushrooms, celery and garlic in a pan and stir in the sherry or wine. Cover and cook over a low heat for 30–40 minutes until the vegetables are tender.

2 Add half the stock and purée in a food processor or blender until smooth. Return to the pan and add the remaining stock, the Worcestershire sauce and nutmeg.

3 Bring to the boil and season to taste with salt and pepper. Serve hot, garnished with celery leaves.

| V |

Mushroom and Bread Soup with Parsley

Thickened with bread, this rich mushroom soup will warm you up on cold winter days. It makes a terrific hearty lunch.

INGREDIENTS

Serves 8

75 g/3 oz/6 tbsp unsalted butter
900 g/2 lb field mushrooms, sliced
2 onions, roughly chopped
600 ml/1 pint/2½ cups milk
8 slices white bread
60 ml/4 tbsp chopped fresh parsley
300 ml/½ pint/1¼ cups double cream
salt and freshly ground black pepper

1 Melt the butter and sauté the sliced mushrooms and chopped onions for about 10 minutes until soft but not browned. Add the milk.

2 Tear the bread into pieces, drop them into the soup and leave to soak for 15 minutes. Purée the soup and return it to the pan. Add 45 ml/3 tbsp of the parsley, the cream and seasoning. Reheat, without boiling. Serve garnished with the remaining parsley.

French Onion Soup

In France, this standard bistro fare is served so frequently that it is simply referred to as gratinée.

INGREDIENTS

Serves 6–8

15 g/½ oz/1 tbsp butter

30 ml/2 tbsp olive oil

4 large onions, finely sliced

2–5 garlic cloves

5 ml/1 tsp sugar

2.5 ml/½ tsp dried thyme

30 ml/2 tbsp plain flour

120 ml/4 fl oz/½ cup dry white wine

2 litres/3½ pints/9 cups beef stock

30 ml/2 tbsp brandy (optional)

6–8 thick slices French bread, toasted

350 g/12 oz/3 cups Gruyère or Emmenthal cheese, grated

1 In a large, heavy saucepan or flameproof casserole, heat the butter and oil over a medium-high heat. Add the onions and cook for 10–12 minutes until they are softened and beginning to brown.

2 Putting one garlic clove aside, finely chop the rest and add to the onions. Add the sugar and thyme and continue cooking over a medium heat for 30–35 minutes until the onions are well browned, stirring frequently.

3 Sprinkle over the flour and stir until well blended. Stir in the wine and stock and bring to the boil. Skim off any foam that rises to the surface, then reduce the heat and simmer gently for 45 minutes. Stir in the brandy, if using.

4 Preheat the grill. Rub each slice of toasted French bread with the remaining garlic clove. Place six or eight ovenproof soup bowls on a baking sheet and fill about three-quarters full with the onion soup.

5 Float a piece of toast in each bowl. Top with grated cheese, dividing it evenly, and grill about 15 cm/6 in from the heat for about 3–4 minutes until the cheese begins to melt and bubble. Serve piping hot.

Spanish Garlic Soup

This is a simple and satisfying soup, made with garlic, which is one of the most popular ingredients in the quick cook's kitchen.

Serves 4

30 ml/2 tbsp olive oil

4 large garlic cloves, peeled

4 slices French bread, about 5 mm/¼ in thick

15 ml/1 tbsp paprika

1 litre/1¾ pints/4 cups beef stock

1.5 ml/¼ tsp ground cumin

a pinch of saffron strands

4 eggs

salt and freshly ground black pepper

chopped fresh parsley, to garnish

1 Preheat the oven to 230°C/ 450°F/Gas 8. Heat the oil in a large pan. Add the whole garlic cloves and cook until golden. Remove and set aside. Fry the bread in the oil until golden, then set aside.

2 Add the paprika to the pan, and fry for a few seconds. Stir in the beef stock, cumin and saffron, then add the reserved garlic, crushing the cloves with the back of a wooden spoon. Season with salt and pepper, then cook for about 5 minutes.

3 Ladle the soup into four ovenproof bowls and break 1 egg into each one. Place a slice of fried bread on top of each egg, then put the bowls in the oven for about 3–4 minutes, until the eggs are set. Sprinkle each portion with parsley and serve at once.

COOK'S TIP

When you switch on the oven, put a baking sheet in at the same time. Stand the soup bowls on the hot baking sheet when you put them in the oven and you will be able to remove them easily when the eggs are set.

Onion and Pancetta Soup

This warming winter soup comes from Umbria, where it is sometimes thickened with beaten eggs and plenty of grated Parmesan cheese. It is then served on top of hot toasted croûtes – rather like savoury scrambled eggs.

Serves 4

115 g/4 oz pancetta rashers, rinds
   removed, roughly chopped
30 ml/2 tbsp olive oil
15 g/¹⁄₂ oz/1 tbsp butter
675 g/1¹⁄₂ lb onions, finely sliced
10 ml/2 tsp granulated sugar
about 1.2 litres/2 pints/5 cups chicken
   stock
350 g/12 oz ripe Italian plum tomatoes,
   peeled and roughly chopped
a few fresh basil leaves, shredded
salt and freshly ground black pepper
grated Parmesan cheese, to serve

1 Put the chopped pancetta in a large saucepan and heat gently, stirring constantly, until the fat runs. Increase the heat to medium, add the oil, butter, sliced onions and sugar and stir well to mix.

2 Half-cover the pan and cook the onions gently for about 20 minutes until golden. Stir frequently and lower the heat if necessary.

3 Add the stock, tomatoes and salt and pepper and bring to the boil, stirring. Lower the heat, half-cover the pan and simmer, stirring occasionally, for about 30 minutes.

4 Check the consistency of the soup and add a little more stock or water if it is too thick.

5 Just before serving, stir in most of the basil and adjust the seasoning to taste. Serve hot, garnished with the remaining shredded basil. Hand round the freshly grated Parmesan separately.

COOK'S TIP

Look for Vidalia onions to make this soup. They are available at large supermarkets, and have a sweet flavour and attractive, yellowish flesh.

V

Spicy Tomato and Coriander Soup

Heartwarming tomato soup is always a favourite. Deliciously spicy, it is also the perfect soup to prepare for a cold winter's day.

INGREDIENTS

Serves 4

675 g/1½ lb tomatoes
30 ml/2 tbsp vegetable oil
1 bay leaf
4 spring onions, chopped
5 ml/1 tsp salt
2.5 ml/½ tsp crushed garlic
5 ml/1 tsp crushed black peppercorns
30 ml/2 tbsp chopped fresh coriander
750 ml/1¼ pints/3 cups water
15 ml/1 tbsp cornflour
30 ml/2 tbsp single cream, to serve

COOK'S TIP

If the only fresh tomatoes available are rather pale and under-ripe, add 15 ml/1 tbsp tomato purée to the pan with the chopped tomatoes. This will enhance the colour and flavour of the soup.

1 To peel the tomatoes, plunge them into very hot water, then lift them out more or less straight away using a slotted spoon. The skin should now peel off quickly and easily. Once this is done, chop the tomatoes roughly.

2 In a medium-size saucepan, heat the oil and fry the chopped tomatoes, bay leaf and chopped spring onions for a few minutes until soft and translucent, but not browned.

3 Gradually add the salt, garlic, peppercorns and fresh coriander to the tomato mixture, finally adding the water.

4 Bring to the boil, lower the heat and simmer for 15–20 minutes. Meanwhile, dissolve the cornflour in a little cold water, and set aside.

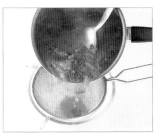

5 Remove the soup from the heat and press through a sieve placed over a bowl. Discard the sieved vegetables.

6 Return to the pan, add the cornflour mixture and stir over a gentle heat for about 3 minutes until thickened.

7 Pour into individual soup bowls and serve piping hot, with a swirl of cream.

Tomato and Vermicelli Soup

*The vermicelli is lightly fried before
being simmered in this tasty soup.*

INGREDIENTS

Serves 4

30 ml/2 tbsp olive or corn oil

50 g/2 oz/¹/₃ cup vermicelli

1 onion, roughly chopped

1 garlic clove, chopped

450 g/1 lb tomatoes, peeled, seeded and
   roughly chopped

1 litre/1³/₄ pints/4 cups chicken stock

1.5 ml/¹/₄ tsp sugar

15 ml/1 tbsp finely chopped fresh
   coriander, plus extra to garnish

salt and freshly ground black pepper

25 g/1 oz/¹/₃ cup grated Parmesan cheese,
   to serve

1 Heat the oil in a frying pan
   and sauté the vermicelli over a
moderate heat until golden brown.
Take care not to let the delicate
strands burn.

2 Remove the pan from the
   heat. Lift out the vermicelli
with a slotted spoon, drain on
kitchen paper and set aside.

3 Purée the onion, garlic and
   tomatoes in a food processor
until smooth. Return the frying
pan to the heat. When the oil is
hot, add the purée. Cook, stirring
constantly, for about 5 minutes or
until thick.

4 Transfer the purée to a
   saucepan. Add the vermicelli
and pour in the stock. Season with
sugar, salt and pepper. Stir in 15 ml/
1 tbsp coriander, bring to the boil,
then lower the heat, cover the pan
and simmer the soup until the
vermicelli is tender.

5 Serve in heated bowls, sprinkle
   with chopped fresh coriander,
and offer the Parmesan separately.

Lightly Spiced Tomato Soup

*Simple and quick to make, this
tomato soup will soon become one of
your firm favourites.*

INGREDIENTS

Serves 4

15 ml/1 tbsp corn or peanut oil

1 onion, finely chopped

900 g/2 lb tomatoes, peeled, seeded and
   chopped

475 ml/16 fl oz/2 cups chicken stock

2 large sprigs of fresh coriander

salt and freshly ground black pepper

coarsely ground black pepper, to serve

1 Heat the oil in a large
   saucepan and gently fry the
onion, stirring frequently, for
about 5 minutes until it is soft and
transparent but not brown.

2 Add the chopped tomatoes,
   chicken stock and coriander to
the pan. Bring to the boil, then
lower the heat, cover the pan and
simmer gently for 15 minutes or
until the tomatoes are soft.

3 Remove and discard the
   coriander. Press the soup
through a sieve and return it to
the clean pan. Season and heat
through. Serve sprinkled with
coarsely ground black pepper.

Broccoli and Bread Soup

Broccoli grows abundantly around Rome and is served in this soup with garlic toasts.

INGREDIENTS

Serves 6

675 g/1½ lb broccoli spears

1.75 litres/3 pints/7½ cups chicken or
    vegetable stock

15 ml/1 tbsp lemon juice

salt and freshly ground black pepper

To serve

6 slices white bread

1 large garlic clove, cut in half

grated Parmesan cheese (optional)

1 Using a small, sharp knife, peel the broccoli stems, starting from the base and pulling gently up towards the florets. (The peel should come off easily.) Chop the broccoli into small chunks.

2 Bring the stock to the boil in a large saucepan. Add the broccoli and simmer for about 10 minutes until soft.

3 Purée about half of the soup and mix into the rest of the soup. Season with salt, pepper and lemon juice.

4 Reheat the soup. Toast the bread, rub with garlic and cut into quarters. Place 3 or 4 pieces of toast in the bottom of each soup plate. Ladle on the soup. Serve at once, with Parmesan if liked.

Tomato and Bread Soup

This colourful Florentine recipe was created to use up stale bread. It can be made with very ripe fresh or canned plum tomatoes.

INGREDIENTS

Serves 4

90 ml/6 tbsp olive oil

small piece dried chilli, crumbled
    (optional)

175 g/6 oz/1½ cups stale bread, cut into
    2.5 cm/1 in cubes

1 medium onion, finely chopped

2 garlic cloves, finely chopped

675 g/1½ lb ripe tomatoes, peeled and
    chopped, or 2 x 400 g/14 oz cans
    peeled plum tomatoes, chopped

45 ml/3 tbsp chopped fresh basil

1.5 litres/2½ pints/6¼ cups light meat
    stock or water, or a combination
    of both

salt and freshly ground black pepper

extra-virgin olive oil, to serve (optional)

1 Heat 60 ml/4 tbsp of the oil in a large saucepan. Add the chilli, if using, and stir for 1–2 minutes. Add the bread cubes and cook until golden, then remove to a plate and drain on kitchen paper.

2 Add the remaining oil, the onion and garlic to the pan and cook until the onion softens. Stir in the tomatoes, basil and the reserved bread cubes. Season with salt. Cook over a moderate heat, stirring occasionally, for about 15 minutes.

3 Meanwhile, heat the stock or water to simmering. Add it to the tomato mixture and stir well. Bring to the boil. Lower the heat slightly and simmer for 20 minutes.

4 Remove the soup from the heat. Use a fork to mash together the tomatoes and bread. Season with pepper, and more salt if necessary. Allow to stand for 10 minutes. Just before serving, swirl in a little extra-virgin olive oil, if liked.

V

Garlicky Lentil Soup

High in fibre, lentils make a particularly tasty soup. Unlike many pulses, they do not need to be soaked before being cooked.

Serves 6

225 g/8 oz/1 cup red lentils, rinsed and
    drained
2 onions, finely chopped
2 large garlic cloves, finely chopped
1 carrot, finely chopped
30 ml/2 tbsp olive oil
2 bay leaves
a generous pinch of dried marjoram or
    oregano
1.5 litres/2½ pints/6¼ cups vegetable
    stock
30 ml/2 tbsp red wine vinegar
salt and freshly ground black pepper
celery leaves, to garnish
crusty bread rolls, to serve

1 Put all the ingredients except for the vinegar, seasoning and garnish in a large, heavy-based saucepan. Bring to the boil over a medium heat, then lower the heat and simmer for 1½ hours, stirring the soup occasionally to prevent the lentils from sticking to the bottom of the pan.

2 Remove the bay leaves and add the red wine vinegar, with salt and pepper to taste. If the soup is too thick, thin it with a little extra vegetable stock or water. Serve the soup in heated bowls, garnished with celery leaves. Serve with warmed crusty rolls.

COOK'S TIP

If you buy your lentils loose, remember to tip them into a sieve or colander and pick them over, removing any pieces of grit, before rinsing them.

Spiced Lentil Soup

V

A subtle blend of spices takes this warming soup to new heights. Serve it with crusty bread for a filling and satisfying lunch.

INGREDIENTS

Serves 6

2 onions, finely chopped

2 garlic cloves, crushed

4 tomatoes, roughly chopped

2.5 ml/½ tsp ground turmeric

5 ml/1 tsp ground cumin

6 cardamom pods

½ cinnamon stick

225 g/8 oz/1 cup red lentils, rinsed and drained

900 ml/1½ pints/3¾ cups water

400 g/14 oz can coconut milk

15 ml/1 tbsp lime juice

salt and freshly ground black pepper

cumin seeds, to garnish

1 Put the onions, garlic, tomatoes, turmeric, cumin, cardamom pods, cinnamon, lentils and water into a saucepan. Bring to the boil, lower the heat, cover and simmer gently for 20 minutes or until the lentils are soft.

2 Remove the cardamom pods and cinnamon stick, then purée the mixture in a blender or food processor. Press the soup through a sieve, then return it to the clean pan.

3 Reserve a little of the coconut milk for the garnish and add the remainder to the pan with the lime juice. Stir well and season with salt and pepper. Reheat the soup gently without boiling. Swirl in the reserved coconut milk, garnish with cumin seeds and serve piping hot.

V

South Indian Pepper Water

This is a highly soothing broth for cold winter evenings. Serve with the whole spices or strain and reheat if you so wish. The lemon juice may be adjusted to taste, but this dish should be distinctly sour.

INGREDIENTS

Serves 2–4

30 ml/2 tbsp vegetable oil

2.5 ml/½ tsp freshly ground black pepper

5 ml/1 tsp cumin seeds

2.5 ml/½ tsp mustard seeds

1.5 ml/¼ tsp asafoetida powder

2 whole dried red chillies

4–6 curry leaves

2.5 ml/½ tsp ground turmeric

2 garlic cloves, crushed

300 ml/½ pint/1¼ cups tomato juice

juice of 2 lemons

120 ml/4 fl oz/½ cup water

salt

fresh coriander leaves, chopped,
   to garnish

1 In a large frying pan, heat the vegetable oil and fry the spices and garlic until the chillies are nearly black and the garlic is a golden brown.

2 Lower the heat and add the tomato juice, lemon juice, water and salt to taste. Bring to the boil, then simmer for 10 minutes. Garnish with chopped coriander and serve piping hot.

COOK'S TIP

Asafoetida is a pungent powder used to enhance Indian vegetarian cooking. In its raw state it can smell quite unpleasant but this smell soon disappears once it is added to your cooking.

Spicy Peanut Soup

*A thick and warming vegetable
soup, excitingly flavoured with chilli
and peanuts.*

INGREDIENTS

Serves 6

30 ml/2 tbsp oil

1 large onion, finely chopped

2 garlic cloves, crushed

5 ml/1 tsp mild chilli powder

2 red peppers, seeded and finely chopped

225 g/8 oz carrots, finely chopped

225 g/8 oz potatoes, finely chopped

3 celery sticks, sliced

900 ml/1½ pints/3¾ cups vegetable stock

90 ml/6 tbsp crunchy peanut butter

115 g/4 oz/⅔ cup sweetcorn

salt and freshly ground black pepper

roughly chopped unsalted roasted
    peanuts, to garnish

1 Heat the oil in a large pan and
cook the onion and garlic for
about 3 minutes. Add the chilli
powder and cook for a further
1 minute.

2 Add the red peppers, carrots,
potatoes and celery. Stir well,
then cook for a further 4 minutes,
stirring occasionally.

3 Add the vegetable stock,
followed by the peanut butter
and sweetcorn. Stir until
thoroughly combined.

4 Season well. Bring to the boil,
cover and simmer for about
20 minutes until all the vegetables
are tender. Adjust the seasoning
before serving, sprinkled with the
chopped peanuts.

Corn and Crab Meat Soup

This soup originated in the USA but it has since been introduced into China. You must use creamed sweetcorn in the recipe to achieve the right consistency.

Serves 4

115 g/4 oz crab meat

2.5 ml/½ tsp finely chopped fresh root
  ginger

30 ml/2 tbsp milk

15 ml/1 tbsp cornflour

2 egg whites

600 ml/1 pint/2½ cups vegetable stock

225 g/8 oz can creamed sweetcorn

salt and freshly ground black pepper

chopped spring onions, to garnish

3 In a wok or saucepan, bring the vegetable stock to the boil. Add the creamed sweetcorn and bring back to the boil once more.

4 Stir in the crab meat and egg white mixture, adjust the seasoning and stir gently until well blended. Serve garnished with chopped spring onions.

1 Flake the crab meat and mix with the ginger in a bowl. In another bowl, mix the milk and cornflour until smooth.

2 Beat the egg whites until frothy, add the milk and cornflour mixture and beat again until smooth. Blend with the crab meat.

VARIATION

If you prefer, you can use coarsely chopped chicken breast instead of crab meat.

Wonton Soup

In China, wonton soup is served as a snack, or dim sum, rather than as a soup course during a large meal.

INGREDIENTS

Serves 4

175 g/6 oz pork, not too lean, roughly
   chopped
50 g/2 oz peeled prawns, finely chopped
5 ml/1 tsp light brown sugar
15 ml/1 tbsp Chinese rice wine or
   dry sherry
15 ml/1 tbsp light soy sauce
5 ml/1 tsp finely chopped spring onions
5 ml/1 tsp finely chopped fresh root ginger
24 ready-made wonton skins
about 750 ml/1¼ pints/3 cups stock
15 ml/1 tbsp light soy sauce
finely chopped spring onions, to garnish

1 In a bowl, thoroughly mix the chopped pork and prawns with the sugar, rice wine or sherry, soy sauce, spring onions and ginger. Set aside for 25–30 minutes for the flavours to blend.

2 Place about 5 ml/1 tsp of the pork mixture in the centre of each wonton skin.

3 Wet the edges of each filled wonton skin with a little water and press them together with your fingers to seal. Fold each wonton parcel over.

4 To cook, bring the stock to a rolling boil in a wok, add the wontons and cook for 4–5 minutes. Season with the soy sauce and add the spring onions.

5 Transfer to individual soup bowls and serve.

HEARTY LUNCH
& SUPPER
SOUPS

~

Winter Vegetable Soup

No fewer than eight varieties of vegetables are packed into this hearty and nutritious soup.

INGREDIENTS

Serves 8

1 medium Savoy cabbage, quartered
    and cored
30 ml/2 tbsp corn oil
4 carrots, finely sliced
2 celery stalks, finely sliced
2 parsnips, diced
1.5 litres/2½ pints/6¼ cups chicken stock
3 medium potatoes, diced
2 courgettes, sliced
1 small red pepper, seeded and diced
115 g/4 oz/2 cups cauliflower florets
2 tomatoes, seeded and diced
2.5 ml/½ tsp fresh thyme leaves or
    1.5 ml/¼ tsp dried thyme
30 ml/2 tbsp chopped fresh parsley
salt and freshly ground black pepper

1 Using a sharp knife, slice the cabbage quarters into thin strips across the leaves.

2 Heat the oil in a large saucepan. Add the cabbage, carrots, celery and parsnips and cook for 10–15 minutes over medium heat, stirring frequently.

3 Stir the stock into the vegetables and bring to the boil, skimming off any foam that rises to the surface.

4 Add the potatoes, courgettes, pepper, cauliflower and tomatoes with the herbs, and salt and pepper to taste. Bring back to the boil. Reduce the heat to low, cover the pan and simmer for 15–20 minutes until the vegetables are tender. Serve hot.

Vegetable and Herb Chowder

V

A medley of fresh vegetables and herbs combines to make a delicious lunchtime soup.

INGREDIENTS

Serves 4

25 g/1 oz/2 tbsp butter
1 onion, finely chopped
1 leek, finely sliced
1 celery stalk, diced
1 yellow or green pepper, seeded and diced
30 ml/2 tbsp chopped fresh parsley
15ml/1 tbsp plain flour
1.2 litres/2 pints/5 cups vegetable stock
350 g/12 oz potatoes, diced
a few sprigs of fresh thyme or 2.5 ml/
    ½ tsp dried thyme
1 bay leaf
115 g/4 oz/1 cup young runner beans,
    thinly sliced on the diagonal
120 ml/4 fl oz/½ cup milk
salt and freshly ground black pepper

1 Melt the butter in a heavy saucepan or flameproof casserole and add the onion, leek, celery, yellow or green pepper and parsley. Cover and cook gently over low heat until the vegetables are soft.

2 Add the flour and stir until well blended. Slowly add the stock, stirring to combine. Bring to the boil, stirring frequently.

3 Add the potatoes, thyme and bay leaf. Simmer, uncovered, for about 10 minutes.

4 Add the beans and simmer for a further 10–15 minutes until all the vegetables are tender.

5 Stir in the milk. Season with salt and pepper. Heat through. Before serving, discard the thyme stalks and bay leaf. Serve hot.

V

Vegetable Soup with Coconut

The coconut gives a delicious flavour to this fine vegetable soup.

Serves 4

25 g/1 oz/2 tbsp butter or margarine

½ red onion, finely chopped

175 g/6 oz each, turnip, sweet potato and
   pumpkin, roughly diced

5 ml/1 tsp dried marjoram

2.5 ml/½ tsp ground ginger

1.5 ml/¼ tsp ground cinnamon

15 ml/1 tbsp chopped spring onion

1 litre/1¾ pints/4 cups well-flavoured
   vegetable stock

30 ml/2 tbsp flaked almonds

1 fresh chilli, seeded and chopped

5 ml/1 tsp sugar

25 g/1 oz creamed coconut

salt and freshly ground black pepper

chopped fresh coriander, to garnish
   (optional)

1 Melt the butter or margarine in a large, non-stick saucepan. Fry the onion for 4–5 minutes. Add the diced vegetables and fry for 3–4 minutes.

2 Add the marjoram, ginger, cinnamon, spring onion and salt and pepper to taste. Fry over a low heat for about 10 minutes, stirring frequently.

3 Add the vegetable stock, flaked almonds, chilli and sugar and stir well to mix. Cover and simmer gently for 10–15 minutes until the vegetables are just tender.

4 Grate the creamed coconut into the soup and stir to mix. Spoon into warmed bowls, sprinkle with chopped coriander, if liked, and serve immediately.

Broad Bean and Rice Soup

V

This thick soup makes the most of fresh broad beans while they are in season. It works well with frozen beans for the rest of the year.

INGREDIENTS

Serves 4

1 kg/2¼ lb broad beans in their pods, or
    400 g/14 oz shelled frozen broad
    beans, thawed
90 ml/6 tbsp olive oil
1 medium onion, finely chopped
2 medium tomatoes, peeled and
    finely chopped
225 g/8 oz/1 cup arborio or other
    non-parboiled rice
25 g/1 oz/2 tbsp butter
1 litre/1¾ pints/4 cups boiling water
salt and freshly ground black pepper
grated Parmesan cheese, to serve
    (optional)

1 Bring a large pan of water to the boil and blanch the beans, fresh or frozen, for 3–4 minutes. Rinse under cold water. If using fresh beans, peel off the skins.

2 Heat the oil in a large saucepan. Add the onion and cook over low to moderate heat until it softens. Stir in the beans and cook for about 5 minutes, stirring to coat them with the oil.

3 Season with salt and pepper. Add the tomatoes and cook for 5 minutes more, stirring often. Add the rice and cook for a further 1–2 minutes, stirring constantly.

4 Add the butter and stir until it melts. Pour in the water, a little at a time. Adjust the seasoning to taste. Continue cooking until the rice is tender. Serve with grated Parmesan, if liked.

V

Fresh Tomato and Bean Soup

This is a rich, chunky tomato soup, with beans and coriander. Serve with olive ciabatta.

INGREDIENTS

Serves 4

900 g/2 lb ripe plum tomatoes

30 ml/2 tbsp olive oil

275 g/10 oz onions, roughly chopped

2 garlic cloves, crushed

900 ml/1½ pints/3¾ cups vegetable stock

30 ml/2 tbsp sun-dried tomato purée

10 ml/2 tsp paprika

15 ml/1 tbsp cornflour

425 g/15 oz can cannellini beans, rinsed
    and drained

30 ml/2 tbsp chopped fresh coriander

salt and freshly ground black pepper

olive ciabatta, to serve

1 First, peel the tomatoes. Using a sharp knife, make a small cross in each one and place in a bowl. Pour over boiling water to cover and leave to stand for 30–60 seconds.

2 Drain the tomatoes and, when they are cool enough to handle, peel off the skins. Quarter them and then cut each piece in half again.

3 Heat the oil in a large saucepan and cook the onions and garlic for 3 minutes or until just beginning to soften.

4 Add the tomatoes to the onions and stir in the stock, sun-dried tomato purée and paprika. Season with a little salt and pepper. Bring to the boil and simmer for 10 minutes.

5 Mix the cornflour to a paste with 30 ml/2 tbsp water. Stir the beans into the soup with the cornflour paste. Cook for a further 5 minutes.

6 Adjust the seasoning and stir in the chopped coriander just before serving with olive ciabatta.

Cauliflower, Flageolet and Fennel Seed Soup

The sweet, anise-liquorice flavour of the fennel seeds gives a delicious edge to this hearty soup.

INGREDIENTS

Serves 4–6

15 ml/1 tbsp olive oil
1 garlic clove, crushed
1 onion, chopped
10 ml/2 tsp fennel seeds
1 cauliflower, cut into small florets
2 x 400 g/14 oz cans flageolet beans, drained and rinsed
1.2 litres/2 pints/5 cups vegetable stock or water
salt and freshly ground black pepper
chopped fresh parsley, to garnish
toasted slices of French bread, to serve

3 Bring the mixture to the boil. Reduce the heat and simmer for about 10 minutes or until the cauliflower is tender. Pour the soup into a blender or food processor and blend until smooth.

4 Stir in the remaining beans and season to taste. Reheat and pour into bowls. Sprinkle with chopped parsley and serve with toasted slices of French bread.

1 Heat the olive oil. Add the garlic, onion and fennel seeds and cook gently for 5 minutes or until softened.

2 Add the cauliflower florets, half the beans and the vegetable stock or water.

Beetroot and Butter Bean Soup

This soup is a simplified version of borscht and is prepared in a fraction of the time. Serve with a spoonful of soured cream and a scattering of chopped fresh parsley.

INGREDIENTS

Serves 4

30 ml/2 tbsp vegetable oil

1 medium onion, sliced

5 ml/1 tsp caraway seeds

finely grated rind of ½ orange

250 g/9 oz cooked beetroot, grated

1.2 litres/2 pints/5 cups beef stock
  or rassol (see Cook's Tip)

400 g/14 oz can butter beans, drained
  and rinsed

15 ml/1 tbsp wine vinegar

60 ml/4 tbsp soured cream

60 ml/4 tbsp chopped fresh parsley,
  to garnish

1 Heat the oil in a large saucepan and cook the onion, caraway seeds and orange rind until soft but not coloured.

2 Add the beetroot, stock or rassol, butter beans and vinegar and simmer on a low heat for a further 10 minutes.

3 Divide the soup between four bowls, add a spoonful of soured cream to each, scatter with chopped parsley and serve.

COOK'S TIP

Rassol is a beetroot broth, which is used to impart a strong beetroot colour and flavour. You are most likely to find it in Kosher food stores.

Spicy Bean Soup

A filling soup made with two kinds of beans flavoured with cumin.

Serves 6–8

175 g/6 oz/1 cup dried black beans, soaked
   overnight and drained
175 g/6 oz/1 cup dried kidney beans,
   soaked overnight and drained
2 bay leaves
90 ml/6 tbsp coarse salt
30 ml/2 tbsp olive or vegetable oil
3 carrots, chopped
1 onion, chopped
1 celery stick
1 garlic clove, crushed
5 ml/1 tsp ground cumin
1.5–2.5 ml/¼–½ tsp cayenne pepper
2.5 ml/½ tsp dried oregano
50 ml/2 fl oz/¼ cup red wine
1.2 litres/2 pints/5 cups beef stock
250 ml/8 fl oz/1 cup water
salt and freshly ground black pepper

For the garnish
soured cream
chopped fresh coriander

1 Put the black beans and kidney beans in two separate pans with cold water to cover and a bay leaf in each. Boil rapidly for 10 minutes, then cover and simmer for 20 minutes.

2 Add 45 ml/3 tbsp coarse salt to each pan and continue simmering for a further 30 minutes until the beans are tender. Drain.

3 Heat the oil in a large flameproof casserole. Add the carrots, onion, celery and garlic and cook over a low heat for 8–10 minutes, stirring, until softened. Stir in the cumin, cayenne, oregano and salt to taste.

4 Add the wine, stock and water and stir to mix all the ingredients together. Remove the bay leaves from the cooked beans and add the beans to the casserole.

5 Bring to the boil, reduce the heat, then cover and simmer for about 20 minutes, stirring occasionally.

6 Transfer half the soup (including most of the solids) to a food processor or blender. Process until smooth. Return to the pan and stir to combine well.

7 Reheat the soup and adjust the seasoning to taste. Serve hot, garnished with soured cream and chopped coriander.

Black and White Bean Soup

V

Although this soup takes a while to prepare, the results are so stunning that it is well worth the effort.

INGREDIENTS

Serves 8

350 g/12 oz/2 cups dried black beans,
    soaked overnight and drained
2.4 litres/4¼ pints/10½ cups water
6 garlic cloves, crushed
350 g/12 oz/2 cups dried white beans,
    soaked overnight and drained
90 ml/6 tbsp balsamic vinegar
4 jalapeño peppers, seeded and chopped
6 spring onions, finely chopped
juice of 1 lime
50 ml/2 fl oz/¼ cup olive oil
15 g/½ oz/¼ cup chopped fresh
    coriander, plus extra to garnish
salt and freshly ground black pepper

1 Place the black beans in a large saucepan with half the water and garlic. Bring to the boil. Reduce the heat to low, cover the pan, and simmer for about 1½ hours until the beans are soft.

2 Meanwhile, put the white beans in another saucepan with the remaining water and garlic. Bring to the boil, cover the pan and simmer for about 1 hour until soft.

3 Purée the cooked white beans in a food processor or blender. Stir in the vinegar, jalapeños, and half the spring onions. Return to the saucepan and reheat gently.

4 Purée the cooked black beans in the food processor or blender. Return to the saucepan and stir in the lime juice, olive oil, coriander and remaining spring onions. Reheat gently.

5 Season both soups with salt and freshly ground black pepper. To serve, place a ladleful of each puréed soup in each soup bowl, side by side. Swirl the two soups together with a cocktail stick or skewer. Garnish with fresh coriander and serve.

V

Pistou

Serve this delicious vegetable soup from Nice, in the south of France, with a sun-dried tomato pesto and fresh Parmesan cheese.

INGREDIENTS

Serves 4

1 courgette, diced
1 small potato, diced
1 shallot, chopped
1 carrot, diced
225 g/8 oz can chopped tomatoes
1.2 litres/2 pints/5 cups vegetable stock
50 g/2 oz French beans, cut into 1 cm/
    ¹/₂ in lengths
50 g/2 oz/¹/₂ cup frozen petits pois
50 g/2 oz/¹/₂ cup small pasta shapes
60–90 ml/4–6 tbsp pesto, either
    home-made or ready-made
15 ml/1 tbsp sun-dried tomato purée
salt and freshly ground black pepper
grated Parmesan cheese, to serve

1 Place the courgette, potato, shallot, carrot and tomatoes in a large pan. Add the vegetable stock and season with salt and pepper. Bring to the boil, then cover and simmer for 20 minutes.

2 Add the French beans, petits pois and pasta shapes. Cook for a further 10 minutes, until the pasta is tender.

3 Taste the soup and adjust the seasoning as necessary. Ladle the soup into individual bowls. Mix together the pesto and sun-dried tomato purée, and stir a spoonful into each serving.

4 Hand round a bowl of grated Parmesan cheese for sprinkling into each bowl.

Ribollita

Ribollita is rather like minestrone, but includes beans instead of pasta. In Italy it is traditionally served ladled over bread and a rich green vegetable, although you could omit this for a lighter version.

INGREDIENTS

Serves 6–8

45 ml/3 tbsp olive oil

2 onions, chopped

2 carrots, sliced

4 garlic cloves, crushed

2 celery sticks, finely sliced

1 fennel bulb, trimmed and chopped

2 large courgettes, finely sliced

400 g/14 oz can chopped tomatoes

30 ml/2 tbsp pesto, either home-made or
  ready-made

900 ml/1½ pints/3¾ cups vegetable stock

400 g/14 oz can haricot or borlotti beans,
  drained

salt and freshly ground black pepper

To serve

450 g/1 lb young spinach

15 ml/1 tbsp extra-virgin olive oil, plus
  extra for drizzling

6–8 slices white bread

Parmesan cheese shavings (optional)

1 Heat the oil in a large saucepan. Add the onions, carrots, garlic, celery and fennel and fry gently for 10 minutes. Add the courgette slices and fry for a further 2 minutes.

2 Add the chopped tomatoes, pesto, stock and beans and bring to the boil. Reduce the heat, cover and simmer gently for 25–30 minutes until all the vegetables are tender. Season with salt and freshly ground black pepper to taste.

3 To serve, fry the spinach in the oil for 2 minutes or until wilted. Spoon over the bread in soup bowls, then ladle the soup over the spinach. Serve with extra olive oil for drizzling on to the soup and Parmesan cheese to sprinkle on top, if liked.

Plantain and Corn Soup

Here the sweetness of the corn and plantains is offset by a little chilli to create an unusual soup.

INGREDIENTS

Serves 4

25 g/1 oz/2 tbsp butter or margarine

1 onion, finely chopped

1 garlic clove, crushed

275 g/10 oz yellow plantains, peeled
 and sliced

1 large tomato, peeled and chopped

175 g/6 oz/1 cup sweetcorn kernels

5 ml/1 tsp dried tarragon, crushed

900 ml/1½ pints/3¾ cups vegetable or
 chicken stock

1 fresh green chilli, seeded and chopped

a pinch of freshly grated nutmeg

salt and freshly ground black pepper

1 Melt the butter or margarine in a saucepan over a moderate heat, add the onion and garlic and fry for a few minutes until the onion is soft.

2 Add the plantains, tomato and sweetcorn kernels, and cook for a further 5 minutes.

3 Add the tarragon, stock, green chilli and salt and freshly ground black pepper, then simmer for 10 minutes or until the plantain is tender. Stir in the grated nutmeg and serve at once.

Groundnut Soup

Groundnuts (or peanuts) are widely used in sauces in African cooking. You'll find groundnut paste in health food shops – it makes a wonderfully rich soup – but you could use peanut butter instead if you prefer.

INGREDIENTS

Serves 4

45 ml/3 tbsp groundnut paste or peanut
 butter

1.5 litres/2½ pints/6¼ cups stock or water

30 ml/2 tbsp tomato purée

1 onion, chopped

2 slices fresh root ginger

1.5ml/¼ tsp dried thyme

1 bay leaf

chilli powder

225 g/8 oz white yam, diced

10 small okras, trimmed (optional)

salt

1 Place the groundnut paste or peanut butter in a bowl, add 300 ml/½ pint/1¼ cups of the stock or water and the tomato purée and blend together to make a smooth paste.

2 Spoon the nut mixture into a saucepan and add the onion, ginger, thyme, bay leaf, chilli powder and salt to taste and the remaining stock.

3 Heat gently until simmering, then cook for 1 hour, whisking from time to time to prevent the nut mixture sticking.

4 Add the white yam, cook for a further 10 minutes, and then add the okra, if using, and simmer until both vegetables are tender. Serve at once.

V

Italian Rocket and Potato Soup

This filling and hearty soup is based on a traditional Italian peasant recipe. If rocket is unavailable, watercress or baby spinach leaves make an equally delicious alternative.

INGREDIENTS

Serves 4

900 g/2 lb new potatoes

900 ml/1½ pints/3¾ cups well-flavoured vegetable stock

1 medium carrot

115 g/4 oz rocket

2.5 ml/½ tsp cayenne pepper

½ loaf stale ciabatta bread, torn into chunks

4 garlic cloves, thinly sliced

60 ml/4 tbsp olive oil

salt and freshly ground black pepper

1 Dice the potatoes, then place them in a saucepan with the stock and a little salt. Bring to the boil and simmer for 10 minutes.

2 Finely dice the carrot and add to the potatoes and stock, then tear the rocket leaves and drop into the pan. Simmer for a further 15 minutes, until the vegetables are tender.

3 Add the cayenne pepper, plus salt and black pepper to taste, then add the chunks of bread. Remove the pan from the heat, cover and leave to stand for about 10 minutes.

4 Meanwhile, sauté the garlic in the olive oil until golden brown. Pour the soup into bowls, add a little of the sautéed garlic to each bowl and serve.

Czech Fish Soup with Dumplings

Use a variety of whatever fish is available in this Czech soup, such as perch, catfish, cod or snapper. The basis of the dumplings is the same whether you use semolina or flour.

INGREDIENTS

Serves 4–8

3 rindless bacon rashers, diced

675 g/1½ lb assorted fresh fish, skinned, boned and diced

15 ml/1 tbsp paprika, plus extra to garnish

1.5 litres/2½ pints/6¼ cups fish stock or water

3 firm tomatoes, peeled and chopped

4 waxy potatoes, peeled and grated

5–10 ml/1–2 tsp chopped fresh marjoram, plus extra to garnish

For the dumplings

75 g/3 oz/½ cup semolina or flour

1 egg, beaten

45 ml/3 tbsp milk or water

generous pinch of salt

15 ml/1 tbsp chopped fresh parsley

1 Dry fry the diced bacon in a large pan until pale golden brown, then add the pieces of assorted fish. Fry for 1–2 minutes, taking care not to break up the pieces of fish.

2 Sprinkle in the paprika, pour in the fish stock or water, bring to the boil and simmer for 10 minutes.

3 Stir the tomatoes, grated potato and marjoram into the pan. Cook for 10 minutes, stirring occasionally.

4 Meanwhile, make the dumplings by mixing all the ingredients together, then leave to stand, covered with clear film, for 5–10 minutes.

5 Drop spoonfuls of the dumpling mixture into the soup and cook for 10 minutes. Serve hot with a little marjoram and paprika.

Yellow Broth

This is one of many versions of this famous Northern Irish soup, which is both thickened with, and given its flavour by, oatmeal.

Serves 4

25 g/1 oz/2 tbsp butter
1 onion, finely chopped
1 celery stick, finely chopped
1 carrot, finely chopped
25 g/1 oz/¼ cup plain flour
900 ml/1½ pints/3¾ cups chicken stock
25 g/1 oz/¼ cup medium oatmeal
115 g/4 oz spinach, chopped
30 ml/2 tbsp cream
salt and freshly ground black pepper
chopped fresh parsley, to garnish
    (optional)

1 Melt the butter in a large saucepan. Add the onion, celery and carrot and cook for about 2 minutes until the onion is beginning to soften.

2 Stir in the flour and cook gently for a further 1 minute, stirring constantly. Pour in the chicken stock, bring to the boil and cover. Reduce the heat and simmer for 30 minutes until the vegetables are tender.

3 Stir in the oatmeal and chopped spinach and cook for a further 15 minutes, stirring from time to time.

4 Stir in the cream and season well. Serve garnished with chopped fresh parsley, if using.

Split Pea and Pumpkin Soup

V

A tasty vegetarian version of a traditional pea soup.

Serves 4

225 g/8 oz/1 cup split peas

1.2 litres/2 pints/5 cups water

25 g/1 oz/2 tbsp butter

1 onion, finely chopped

225 g/8 oz pumpkin, chopped

3 tomatoes, peeled and chopped

5 ml/1 tsp dried tarragon, crushed

15 ml/1 tbsp chopped fresh coriander

2.5 ml/½ tsp ground cumin

1 vegetable stock cube, crumbled

chilli powder, to taste

sprigs of fresh coriander, to garnish

1 Soak the split peas overnight in enough water to cover them completely, then drain. Place the split peas in a large saucepan, add the water and boil for about 30 minutes until tender.

2 In a separate pan, melt the butter and sauté the onion until soft but not browned.

3 Add the pumpkin, tomatoes, tarragon, coriander, cumin, vegetable stock cube and chilli powder and, on a high heat, bring to the boil.

4 Stir the vegetable mixture into the cooked split peas and their liquid. Simmer gently for about 20 minutes or until the vegetables are tender. If the soup is too thick, add another 150 ml/¼ pint/⅔ cup water. Serve hot, garnished with sprigs of coriander.

V

Green Lentil Soup

Lentil soup is an eastern Mediterranean classic, varying in its spiciness according to region. Red or puy lentils make an equally good substitute for the green lentils used in this version.

INGREDIENTS

Serves 4-6

225 g/8 oz/1 cup green lentils

75 ml/5 tbsp olive oil

3 onions, finely chopped

2 garlic cloves, finely sliced

10 ml/2 tsp cumin seeds, crushed

1.5 ml/¼ tsp ground turmeric

600 ml/1 pint/2½ cups vegetable stock

600 ml/1 pint/2½ cups water

salt and freshly ground black pepper

30 ml/2 tbsp roughly chopped fresh
    coriander, to garnish

warm crusty bread, to serve

1 Put the lentils in a saucepan and cover with cold water. Bring to the boil and boil rapidly for 10 minutes. Drain.

2 Heat 30 ml/2 tbsp of the oil in a pan and fry 2 of the onions with the garlic, cumin and turmeric for 3 minutes, stirring. Add the lentils, stock and water. Bring to the boil, reduce the heat, cover and simmer for 30 minutes until the lentils are soft.

3 Heat the remaining oil and fry the third onion until golden brown, stirring frequently.

4 Use a potato masher to lightly mash the lentils and make the soup pulpy in texture. Reheat gently and season with salt and freshly ground pepper to taste.

5 Pour the soup into bowls. Stir the fresh coriander in with the fried onion and scatter over the soup as a garnish. Serve with warm crusty bread.

COOK'S TIP

The lentils do not need to be soaked before cooking.

Lentil Soup with Rosemary

*A classic rustic Italian soup
flavoured with rosemary, this is
delicious served with garlic bread.*

INGREDIENTS

Serves 4

225 g/8 oz/1 cup dried green or brown
  lentils
45 ml/3 tbsp extra-virgin olive oil
3 rindless streaky bacon rashers, cut into
  small dice
1 onion, finely chopped
2 celery sticks, finely chopped
2 carrots, finely chopped
2 sprigs of fresh rosemary, finely
  chopped
2 bay leaves
400 g/14 oz can plum tomatoes
1.75 litres/3 pints/7½ cups vegetable stock
salt and freshly ground black pepper
fresh bay leaves and sprigs of fresh
  rosemary, to garnish

1 Place the lentils in a bowl and
cover with cold water. Leave to
soak for at least 2 hours. Rinse and
drain well.

2 Heat the oil in a large
saucepan. Add the bacon and
cook for about 3 minutes, then
stir in the onion and cook for 5
minutes until softened. Stir in
the celery, carrots, rosemary,
bay leaves and lentils. Toss over
the heat for 1 minute until
thoroughly coated in the oil.

3 Tip in the tomatoes and stock,
and bring to the boil. Lower
the heat, half-cover the pan and
simmer for about 1 hour until the
lentils are perfectly tender.

4 Remove the bay leaves, add
salt and freshly ground black
pepper to taste and serve with a
garnish of fresh bay leaves and
sprigs of rosemary.

COOK'S TIP

Look out for the small
green lentils in Italian groceries
or delicatessens.

V

Lentil and Pasta Soup

This rustic vegetarian soup makes a filling lunch or supper and goes well with granary or crusty Italian bread.

INGREDIENTS

Serves 4–6

175 g/6 oz/³⁄₄ cup brown lentils

3 garlic cloves

1 litre/1³⁄₄ pints/4 cups water

45 ml/3 tbsp olive oil

25 g/1 oz/2 tbsp butter

1 onion, finely chopped

2 celery sticks, finely chopped

30 ml/2 tbsp sun-dried tomato purée

1.75 litres/3 pints/7¹⁄₂ cups vegetable stock

a few fresh marjoram leaves, plus extra
   to garnish

a few fresh basil leaves

leaves from 1 sprig of fresh thyme

50 g/2 oz/¹⁄₂ cup small pasta shapes,
   such as tubetti

salt and freshly ground black pepper

1 Put the lentils in a large saucepan. Smash one of the garlic cloves (there's no need to peel it first) and add it to the lentils. Pour in the water and bring to the boil. Lower the heat to a gentle simmer and cook for about 20 minutes, stirring occasionally, until the lentils are just tender.

2 Tip the lentils into a sieve, remove the cooked garlic clove and set it aside.

3 Rinse the lentils under the cold tap, then leave them to drain. Heat 30 ml/2 tbsp of the oil with half of the butter in a large saucepan. Add the onion and celery and cook over a low heat, stirring frequently, for 5–7 minutes until softened.

COOK'S TIP

Use green lentils instead of brown, if you like, but the orange or red ones are not so good for this soup because they tend to go mushy.

4 Crush the remaining garlic and peel and mash the reserved cooked garlic clove. Add to the vegetables with the remaining oil, the tomato purée and lentils. Stir, then add the stock, herbs and salt and pepper to taste. Bring to the boil, stirring. Simmer for 30 minutes, stirring occasionally.

5 Add the pasta and bring to the boil, stirring. Simmer, stirring frequently, for 7–8 minutes or according to the instructions on the packet, until the pasta is *al dente*. Add the remaining butter and adjust the seasoning. Serve hot in warmed bowls, garnished with marjoram leaves.

Roasted Tomato and Pasta Soup

V

When the only tomatoes you can buy are not particularly flavoursome, make this soup. The roasting compensates for any lack of flavour in the tomatoes, and the soup has a wonderful, smoky taste.

INGREDIENTS

Serves 4

450 g/1 lb ripe Italian plum tomatoes, halved lengthways

1 large red pepper, quartered lengthways and seeded

1 large red onion, quartered lengthways

2 garlic cloves, unpeeled

15 ml/1 tbsp olive oil

1.2 litres/2 pints/5 cups vegetable stock or water

a good pinch of granulated sugar

90 g/3½ oz/scant 1 cup small pasta shapes, such as tubetti or small macaroni

salt and freshly ground black pepper

fresh basil leaves, to garnish

1 Preheat the oven to 190°C/ 375°F/Gas 5. Spread out the tomatoes, red pepper, onion and garlic in a roasting tin and drizzle with the olive oil. Roast for 30–40 minutes until the vegetables are soft and charred, stirring and turning them halfway through cooking.

2 Tip the vegetables into a food processor, add about 250 ml/ 8 fl oz/1 cup of the stock or water, and process until puréed. Scrape into a sieve placed over a large saucepan and press the purée through into the pan.

3 Add the remaining stock or water, the sugar and salt and pepper to taste. Bring to the boil.

4 Add the pasta and simmer for 7–8 minutes (or according to the instructions on the packet), stirring frequently, until *al dente*. Taste and adjust the seasoning with salt and freshly ground black pepper. Serve hot in warmed bowls, garnished with the fresh basil leaves.

COOK'S TIP

You can roast the vegetables in advance, allow them to cool, then leave them in a covered bowl in the refrigerator overnight before puréeing.

Tiny Pasta in Broth

In Italy this soup is often served with bread for a light supper.

INGREDIENTS

Serves 4

1.2 litres/2 pints/5 cups beef stock

75 g/3 oz/³⁄₄ cup small soup pasta, such as stellette

2 pieces bottled roasted red pepper (about 50 g/2 oz)

salt and freshly ground black pepper

grated Parmesan cheese, to serve

1 Bring the beef stock to the boil in a large saucepan. Add salt and pepper to taste, then drop in the soup pasta. Stir well and bring the stock back to the boil.

2 Lower the heat to a simmer and cook for 7–8 minutes or according to the packet instructions, until the pasta is *al dente*. Stir often during cooking to prevent the pasta shapes sticking together.

3 Drain the pieces of bottled roasted pepper and dice them finely. Place them in the bottom of four warmed soup plates, and set them aside.

4 Taste the soup and adjust the seasoning. Ladle into the soup plates and serve immediately, with grated Parmesan handed round separately.

Little Stuffed Hats in Broth

This soup is served in northern Italy on Santo Stefano (St Stephen's Day – our Boxing Day) and on New Year's Day. It makes a welcome change from all the special celebration food, the day before. It is traditionally made with the Christmas capon carcass, but chicken stock works equally well.

INGREDIENTS

Serves 4

1.2 litres/2 pints/5 cups chicken stock

90–115 g/3¹⁄₂–4 oz/1 cup fresh or dried cappelletti

30 ml/2 tbsp dry white wine (optional)

about 15 ml/1 tbsp finely chopped fresh flat-leaf parsley (optional)

salt and freshly ground black pepper

about 30 ml/2 tbsp grated Parmesan cheese, to serve

1 Pour the chicken stock into a large saucepan and bring to the boil. Add a little salt and pepper to taste, then drop in the pasta.

2 Stir well and bring back to the boil. Lower the heat to a simmer and cook according to the instructions on the packet, until the pasta is *al dente*. Stir frequently during cooking to ensure the pasta cooks evenly.

3 Swirl in the wine and parsley, if using, then taste and adjust the seasoning. Ladle into four warmed soup plates, then sprinkle with grated Parmesan. Serve immediately.

COOK'S TIP

Cappelletti is just another name for tortellini, which come from Romagna. You can either buy them ready-made or make your own.

Pasta and Chick-pea Soup

This is a simple, country-style, filling soup. The shape of the pasta and the beans complement one another beautifully.

INGREDIENTS

Serves 4–6

60 ml/4 tbsp olive oil

1 onion, finely chopped

2 carrots, finely chopped

2 celery sticks, finely chopped

400 g/14 oz can chick-peas, rinsed
    and drained

200 g/7 oz can cannellini beans, rinsed
    and drained

150 ml/¼ pint/⅔ cup passata

120 ml/4 fl oz/½ cup water

1.5 litres/2½ pints/6¼ cups vegetable or
    chicken stock

1 sprig of fresh rosemary, plus a few leaves
    to garnish

200 g/7 oz/scant 2 cups dried conchiglie

salt and freshly ground black pepper

shavings of Parmesan cheese, to serve

1 Heat the oil in a large saucepan, add the chopped vegetables and cook over a low heat, stirring frequently, for 5–7 minutes.

2 Add the chick-peas and cannellini beans, stir well to mix, then cook for 5 minutes. Stir in the passata and water. Cook, stirring, for 2–3 minutes.

3 Add 475 ml/16 fl oz/2 cups of the stock, the rosemary sprig and salt and freshly ground black pepper to taste. Bring to the boil, cover, then simmer gently, stirring occasionally, for 1 hour.

VARIATIONS

You can use other pasta shapes, but conchiglie are ideal because they scoop up the chick-peas and beans. Crush 1–2 garlic cloves and fry them with the vegetables, if you like.

---

4 Pour in the remaining stock, add the pasta and bring to the boil. Lower the heat and simmer for 7–8 minutes (or according to the instructions on the packet), until the pasta is *al dente*. Remove the rosemary sprig. Serve the soup sprinkled with rosemary leaves and Parmesan shavings.

Chick-pea and Parsley Soup

Parsley and a hint of lemon bring freshness to chick-peas.

Serves 6

225 g/8 oz/1⅓ cups chick-peas,
  soaked overnight
1 small onion
1 bunch of fresh parsley (about 40 g/1½ oz
30 ml/2 tbsp olive and sunflower
  oils, mixed
1.2 litres/2 pints/5 cups chicken stock
juice of ½ lemon
salt and freshly ground black pepper
lemon wedges and finely pared strips of
  rind, to garnish

3 Heat the olive and sunflower oils in a saucepan or flame-proof casserole and fry the onion mixture for about 4 minutes over a low heat until the onion is slightly softened.

4 Add the chick-peas, cook gently for 1–2 minutes then add the stock. Season well. Bring the soup to the boil, then cover and simmer for 20 minutes.

5 Allow the soup to cool a little and then mash the chick-peas with a fork until the soup is thick but still quite chunky.

6 Reheat the soup and add the lemon juice. Serve garnished with lemon wedges and rind.

1 Drain the chick-peas and rinse under cold water. Cook them in boiling water for 1–1½ hours until tender. Drain and peel.

2 Place the onion and parsley in a food processor or blender and process until finely chopped.

Chick-pea and Spinach Soup with Garlic

This delicious, thick and creamy soup is richly flavoured and perfect for vegetarians.

INGREDIENTS

Serves 4

30 ml/2 tbsp olive oil

4 garlic cloves, crushed

1 onion, roughly chopped

10 ml/2 tsp ground cumin

10 ml/2 tsp ground coriander

1.2 litres/2 pints/5 cups vegetable stock

350 g/12 oz potatoes, finely chopped

425 g/15 oz can chick-peas, drained

15 ml/1 tbsp cornflour

150 ml/¼ pint/⅔ cup double cream

30 ml/2 tbsp light tahini

200 g/7 oz spinach, shredded

cayenne pepper

salt and freshly ground black pepper

2 Stir in the ground cumin and coriander and cook for 1 minute. Add the stock and potatoes. Bring to the boil and simmer for 10 minutes.

3 Add the chick-peas and simmer for a further 5 minutes or until the potatoes are just tender.

4 Blend together the cornflour, cream, tahini and plenty of seasoning. Stir into the soup with the spinach. Bring to the boil, stirring, and simmer for a further 2 minutes. Adjust the seasoning with salt, pepper and cayenne pepper to taste. Serve sprinkled with a little extra cayenne pepper.

1 Heat the oil in a large saucepan and cook the garlic and onion for about 5 minutes or until the onion is softened and golden brown.

COOK'S TIP

Tahini is sesame seed paste and is available from many health food shops.

Eastern European Chick-pea Soup

Chick-peas form part of the staple diet in the Balkans, where this soup originates. It is economical to make, and is a hearty and satisfying dish.

INGREDIENTS

Serves 4–6

500 g/1¼ lb/5 cups chick-peas, soaked overnight

2 litres/3½ pints/9 cups vegetable stock

3 large waxy potatoes, cut into bite-size chunks

50 ml/2 fl oz/¼ cup olive oil

225 g/8 oz spinach leaves

salt and freshly ground black pepper

spicey sausage, cooked (optional)

1 Drain the chick-peas and rinse under cold water. Place in a large pan with the vegetable stock. Bring to the boil, then reduce the heat and cook gently for about one hour.

2 Add the potatoes, olive oil and salt and pepper to taste. Cook for 20 minutes until the potatoes are tender.

3 Add the spinach and sliced, cooked sausage (if using) 5 minutes before the end of cooking. Serve the soup in individual warmed soup bowls.

Sweetcorn and Scallop Chowder

Fresh sweetcorn is ideal for this chowder, although canned or frozen sweetcorn also works well. This soup is almost a meal in itself and makes a perfect lunch dish.

INGREDIENTS

Serves 4–6

2 sweetcorn cobs or 200 g/7 oz/generous
   1 cup frozen or canned sweetcorn
600 ml/1 pint/2½ cups milk
15 g/½ oz butter or margarine
1 small leek or onion, chopped
40 g/1½ oz/¼ cup smoked streaky bacon,
   finely chopped
1 small garlic clove, crushed
1 small green pepper, seeded and diced
1 celery stick, chopped
1 medium potato, diced
15 ml/1 tbsp plain flour
300 ml/½ pint/1¼ cups chicken or
   vegetable stock
4 scallops
115 g/4 oz cooked fresh mussels
a pinch of paprika
150 ml/¼ pint/⅔ cup single cream
   (optional)
salt and freshly ground black pepper

1 Using a sharp knife, slice down the corn cobs to remove the kernels. Place half the kernels in a food processor or blender and process with a little of the milk. Set the other half aside.

2 Melt the butter or margarine in a large saucepan and gently fry the leek or onion, bacon and garlic for 4–5 minutes until the leek is soft but not browned. Add the green pepper, celery and potato and sweat over a gentle heat for a further 3–4 minutes, stirring frequently.

3 Stir in the flour and cook for about 1–2 minutes until golden and frothy. Stir in a little milk and the corn mixture, stock, the remaining milk and corn kernels and seasoning.

4 Bring to the boil, and then simmer, partially covered, for 15–20 minutes until the vegetables are tender.

5 Pull the corals away from the scallops and slice the white flesh into 5 mm/¼ in slices. Stir the scallops into the soup, cook for 4 minutes and then stir in the corals, mussels and paprika. Heat through for a few minutes and then stir in the cream, if using. Check the seasoning and serve.

Clam Chowder

A traditional chowder from New England in the United States of America, the mixture of clams and pork, with potatoes and cream, is rich and utterly delicious.

INGREDIENTS

Serves 8

48 clams, scrubbed
1.5 litres/2½ pints/6¼ cups water
40 g/1½ oz/¼ cup finely diced salt pork
    or bacon
3 medium onions, finely chopped
1 bay leaf
3 medium potatoes, diced
475 ml/16 fl oz/2 cups milk, warmed
250 ml/8 fl oz/1 cup single cream
salt and freshly ground black pepper
chopped fresh parsley, to garnish

1 Rinse the clams well in cold water. Drain. Place them in a deep pan with the water and bring to the boil. Cover and steam for about 10 minutes until the shells open. Remove from the heat.

2 When the clams have cooled slightly, remove them from their shells. Discard any clams that have not opened. Chop the clams coarsely. Strain the cooking liquid through a sieve lined with muslin and reserve.

3 In a large, heavy saucepan, fry the salt pork or bacon until it renders its fat and begins to brown. Add the onions and cook over a low heat for 8–10 minutes until softened.

4 Stir in the bay leaf, potatoes, and clam cooking liquid. Bring to the boil and cook for 5–10 minutes.

5 Stir in the chopped clams. Continue to cook until the potatoes are tender, stirring from time to time. Season.

6 Stir in the warmed milk and cream and heat very gently for a further 5 minutes. Discard the bay leaf, adjust the seasoning and serve sprinkled with chopped fresh parsley.

Spiced Mussel Soup

*Chunky and colourful, this Turkish
fish soup is like a chowder in its
consistency. It is flavoured with
harissa sauce, which is more
familiar in north African cookery.*

INGREDIENTS

Serves 6

1.5 kg/3–3½ lb fresh mussels
150 ml/¼ pint/⅔ cup white wine
30 ml/2 tbsp olive oil
1 onion, finely chopped
2 garlic cloves, crushed
2 celery sticks, finely sliced
bunch of spring onions, finely sliced
1 potato, diced
7.5 ml/1½ tsp harissa sauce
3 tomatoes, peeled and diced
45 ml/3 tbsp chopped fresh parsley
freshly ground black pepper
thick natural yogurt, to serve (optional)

1 Scrub the mussels, discarding
any damaged ones or any
open ones that do not close when
tapped with a knife.

2 Bring the wine to the boil in a
large saucepan. Add the
mussels and cover with a lid. Cook
for 4–5 minutes until the mussels
have opened wide. Discard any
mussels that remain closed. Drain
the mussels, reserving the cooking
liquid. Reserve a few mussels in
their shells to use as a garnish and
shell the rest.

3 Heat the oil in a pan and fry
the onion, garlic, celery and
spring onions for 5 minutes.

4 Add the shelled mussels,
reserved liquid, potato, harissa
sauce and tomatoes. Bring to the
boil, reduce the heat and cover.
Simmer gently for 25 minutes or
until the potatoes are breaking up.

5 Stir in the parsley and pepper
and add the reserved mussels
in their shells. Heat through for
1 minute. Serve hot with a spoonful
of yogurt, if liked.

Curried Salmon Soup

A hint of mild curry paste really enhances the flavour of this soup, without making it too spicy.

INGREDIENTS

Serves 4

50 g/2 oz/4 tbsp butter
225 g/8 oz onions, roughly chopped
10 ml/2 tsp mild curry paste
475 ml/16 fl oz/2 cups water
150 ml/¼ pint/⅔ cup white wine
300 ml/½ pint/1¼ cups double cream
50 g/2 oz/½ cup creamed coconut, grated
350 g/12 oz potatoes, finely chopped
450 g/1 lb salmon fillet, skinned and cut
    into bite-size pieces
60 ml/4 tbsp chopped fresh flat-leaf parsley
salt and freshly ground black pepper

3 Add the potatoes to the pan and simmer, covered, for about 15 minutes, or until they are almost tender. Do not allow them to break down into the mixture.

4 Stir in the fish gently so as not to break it up. Simmer for 2–3 minutes until just tender. Add the parsley and adjust the seasoning. Serve immediately.

1 Melt the butter in a large saucepan, add the onions and cook over a low heat for about 3–4 minutes until beginning to soften. Add the curry paste and cook for 1 minute further.

2 Add the water, wine, cream, creamed coconut and a little seasoning. Bring to the boil, stirring, until the coconut has dissolved smoothly.

Salmon Chowder

Dill is the perfect partner for salmon in this creamy soup.

INGREDIENTS

Serves 4

20 g/³⁄₄ oz/1¹⁄₂ tbsp butter or margarine
1 onion, finely chopped
1 leek, finely chopped
1 small fennel bulb, finely chopped
25 g/1 oz/¹⁄₄ cup flour
1.75 litres/3 pints/7¹⁄₂ cups fish stock
2 medium potatoes, cut in 1 cm/¹⁄₂ in cubes
450 g/1 lb boneless, skinless salmon, cut in
   2 cm/³⁄₄ in cubes
175 ml/6 fl oz/³⁄₄ cup milk
120 ml/4 fl oz/¹⁄₂ cup whipping cream
30 g/2 tbsp chopped fresh dill
salt and freshly ground black pepper

1 Melt the butter or margarine in a large saucepan. Add the onion, leek and chopped fennel and cook over a medium heat for 5–8 minutes until softened, stirring from time to time.

2 Stir in the flour. Reduce the heat to low and cook for 3 minutes, stirring occasionally.

3 Add the fish stock and potatoes. Season with salt and ground black pepper. Bring to the boil, then reduce the heat, cover and simmer for about 20 minutes or until the potatoes are tender.

4 Add the salmon and simmer gently for 3–5 minutes until it is just cooked.

5 Stir in the milk, cream, and dill. Cook until just warmed through, but do not boil. Adjust the seasoning and then serve.

Smoked Haddock and Potato Soup

The proper name for this traditional Scottish soup is cullen skink. *A* cullen *is the seatown or port district of a town, while* skink *means stock or broth.*

Serves 6

1 Finnan haddock, about 350 g/12 oz

1 onion, chopped

1 bouquet garni

900 ml/1½ pints/3¾ cups water

500 g/1¼ lb potatoes, quartered

600 ml/1 pint/2½ cups milk

40 g/1½ oz/3 tbsp butter

salt and freshly ground black pepper

snipped fresh chives, to garnish

crusty bread, to serve

1 Put the haddock, onion, bouquet garni and water into a large saucepan and bring to the boil. Skim the scum from the surface, then cover the pan. Reduce the heat and poach for 10–15 minutes, until the haddock flakes easily.

2 Lift the haddock from the pan, using a fish slice, and remove the skin and bones. Flake the flesh and reserve. Return the skin and bones to the pan and simmer, uncovered, for 30 minutes. Strain the stock through a sieve.

3 Return the stock to the pan, then add the potatoes and simmer for about 25 minutes, or until tender. Remove the potatoes from the pan using a slotted spoon. Add the milk to the pan and bring to the boil.

4 Meanwhile, mash the potatoes with the butter, then whisk into the liquid in the pan until thick and creamy. Add the flaked fish to the pan and adjust the seasoning. Sprinkle with chives and serve at once with crusty bread.

Smoked Cod and Okra Soup

The inspiration for this soup came from a Ghanaian recipe for okra soup. Here it is enhanced by the addition of smoked fish.

Serves 4

2 green bananas

50 g/2 oz/4 tbsp butter or margarine

1 onion, finely chopped

2 tomatoes, peeled and finely chopped

115 g/4 oz okra, trimmed

225 g/8 oz smoked cod fillet, cut into bite-size pieces

900 ml/1½ pints/3¾ cups fish stock

1 fresh chilli, seeded and chopped

salt and freshly ground black pepper

sprigs of fresh parsley, to garnish

3 Add the cod, fish stock, chilli and seasoning. Bring to the boil, then reduce the heat and simmer for about 20 minutes or until the cod is cooked through and flakes easily.

4 Peel the cooked bananas and cut into slices. Stir into the soup, heat through for a few minutes and ladle into soup bowls. Garnish with parsley and serve.

1 Slit the skins of the green bananas and place in a large saucepan. Cover with water, bring to the boil and cook over a moderate heat for 25 minutes until the bananas are tender. Transfer to a plate and leave to cool.

2 Melt the butter or margarine in a large saucepan and sauté the onion for about 5 minutes until soft. Stir in the chopped tomatoes and okra and fry gently for a further 10 minutes.

Fish Ball Soup

The Japanese name for this soup is Tsumire-jiru. Tsumire, *means, quite literally, sardine balls, and these are added to this delicious soup to impart their robust flavour.*

INGREDIENTS

Serves 4

100 ml/3½ fl oz/generous ⅓ cup sake or
    dry white wine
1.2 litres/2 pints/5 cups instant dashi
60 ml/4 tbsp white miso paste
150 g/5 oz shimeji mushrooms or
    6 shiitake mushrooms
1 leek or large spring onion

For the fish balls

20 g/¾ oz fresh root ginger
800 g/1¾ lb fresh sardines, gutted and
    heads removed
30 ml/2 tbsp white miso paste
15 ml/1 tbsp sake or dry white wine
7.5 ml/1½ tsp sugar
1 egg
30 ml/2 tbsp cornflour

1 First make the fish balls. To do this, grate the ginger and squeeze it well to yield 5 ml/1 tsp ginger juice.

2 Rinse the sardines under cold running water, then cut in half along the backbone. Remove all the bones. To skin a boned sardine, lay it skin-side down on a board, then run a sharp knife slowly along the skin from tail to head.

3 Coarsely chop the sardines and process with the ginger juice, miso, sake or wine, sugar and egg to a thick paste in a food processor or blender. Transfer to a bowl and mix in the cornflour until thoroughly blended.

4 Trim the shimeji mushrooms and either separate each stem or remove the stems from the shiitake mushrooms and shred them. Cut the leek or spring onion into 4 cm/1½ in strips.

5 Bring the ingredients for the soup to the boil. Use 2 wet spoons to shape small portions of the sardine mixture into bite-size balls and drop them into the soup. Add the prepared mushrooms and leek or spring onion.

6 Simmer the soup until the sardine balls float to the surface. Serve immediately, in individual, deep soup bowls.

Chicken Minestrone

This is a special minestrone made with fresh chicken. Served with crusty Italian bread, it makes a hearty meal in itself.

INGREDIENTS

Serves 4–6

15 ml/1 tbsp olive oil

2 chicken thighs

3 rindless streaky bacon rashers, chopped

1 onion, finely chopped

a few fresh basil leaves, shredded

a few fresh rosemary leaves, finely chopped

15 ml/1 tbsp chopped fresh flat-leaf parsley

2 potatoes, cut into 1 cm/½ in cubes

1 large carrot, cut into 1 cm/½ in cubes

2 small courgettes, cut into 1 cm/½ in cubes

1–2 celery sticks, cut into 1cm/½in cubes

1 litre/1¾ pints/4 cups chicken stock

200 g/7 oz/1¾ cups frozen peas

90 g/3½ oz/scant 1 cup stellette or other small soup pasta

salt and freshly ground black pepper

Parmesan cheese shavings, to serve

1 Heat the oil in a large frying pan, add the chicken thighs and fry for about 5 minutes on each side. Remove with a slotted spoon and set aside.

2 Add the bacon, onion and herbs to the pan and cook gently, stirring constantly, for about 5 minutes. Add the potatoes, carrot, courgettes and celery and cook for 5–7 minutes more.

3 Return the chicken thighs to the pan, add the stock and bring to the boil. Cover and cook over a low heat for 35–40 minutes, stirring the soup occasionally.

4 Remove the chicken thighs with a slotted spoon and place them on a board. Stir the peas and pasta into the soup and bring back to the boil. Simmer, stirring frequently, for 7–8 minutes or according to the instructions on the packet, until the pasta is just *al dente*.

5 Meanwhile, remove and discard the chicken skin, then remove the meat from the chicken bones and cut it into small (1 cm/½ in) pieces.

6 Return the meat to the soup, stir well and heat through. Taste and adjust the seasoning as necessary.

7 Serve hot in warmed soup plates or bowls, topped with Parmesan shavings.

Pasta Squares and Peas in Broth

This thick soup is from Lazio, where it is traditionally made with fresh home-made pasta and peas. In this modern version, ready-made pasta is used with frozen peas to save time.

INGREDIENTS

Serves 4–6

25 g/1 oz/2 tbsp butter

50 g/2 oz/¹/₃ cup pancetta or rindless
    smoked streaky bacon, roughly
    chopped

1 small onion, finely chopped

1 celery stick, finely chopped

400 g/14 oz/3¹/₂ cups frozen peas

5 ml/1 tsp tomato purée

5–10 ml/1–2 tsp finely chopped fresh
    flat-leaf parsley

1 litre/1³/₄ pints/4 cups chicken stock

300 g/11 oz fresh lasagne sheets

about 50 g/2 oz/¹/₃ cup prosciutto or
    Parma ham, cut into cubes

salt and freshly ground black pepper

grated Parmesan cheese, to serve

1 Melt the butter in a large
saucepan and add the pancetta
or bacon, with the onion and
celery. Cook over a low heat,
stirring constantly, for 5 minutes.

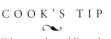

COOK'S TIP

Take care when adding salt
because of the saltiness of the
pancetta and the prosciutto.

2 Add the peas and cook,
stirring, for 3–4 minutes. Stir
in the tomato purée and parsley,
then add the stock, with salt and
pepper to taste. Bring to the boil.
Cover the pan, lower the heat and
simmer gently for 10 minutes.
Meanwhile, cut the lasagne sheets
into 2 cm/³/₄ in squares.

3 Taste the soup and adjust the
seasoning. Drop in the pasta,
stir and bring to the boil. Simmer
for 2–3 minutes or until the
pasta is *al dente*, then stir in the
ham. Serve hot in warmed bowls,
with grated Parmesan handed
round separately.

Squash, Bacon and Swiss Cheese Soup

This is a lightly spiced squash soup, enriched with plenty of creamy melting cheese.

INGREDIENTS

Serves 4

900 g/2 lb butternut squash
225 g/8 oz smoked back bacon
15 ml/1 tbsp oil
225 g/8 oz onions, roughly chopped
2 garlic cloves, crushed
10 ml/2 tsp ground cumin
15 ml/1 tbsp ground coriander
275 g/10 oz potatoes, cut into small
   chunks
900 ml/1½ pints/3¾ cups vegetable stock
10 ml/2 tsp cornflour
30 ml/2 tbsp crème fraîche
Tabasco sauce, to taste
salt and freshly ground black pepper
175 g/6 oz/1½ cups Gruyère cheese,
   grated, to serve
crusty bread to serve

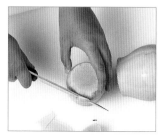

1   Cut the squash into large pieces. Using a sharp knife, carefully remove the skin, wasting as little flesh as possible.

2   Scoop out and discard the seeds. Chop the squash into small chunks. Remove all the fat from the bacon and roughly chop it into small pieces.

3   Heat the oil in a large saucepan and cook the onions and garlic for 3 minutes, or until beginning to soften.

4   Add the bacon and cook for about 3 minutes. Stir in the spices and cook on a low heat for a further minute.

5   Add the chopped squash, potatoes and stock. Bring to the boil and simmer for 15 minutes, or until the squash and potatoes are tender.

6   Blend the cornflour with 30 ml/2 tbsp water and add to the soup with the crème fraîche. Bring to the boil and simmer, uncovered, for 3 minutes. Adjust the seasoning and add Tabasco sauce to taste.

7   Ladle the soup into warm bowls and sprinkle the cheese on top. Serve immediately with crusty bread to scoop up the melted cheese.

COOK'S TIP
~
Pumpkin can be used instead of butternut squash and is equally delicious.

Split Pea and Ham Soup

The main ingredient for this dish is bacon hock, which is the narrow piece of bone cut from a leg of ham. You could use a piece of pork belly instead, if you prefer, and remove it with the herbs before serving.

INGREDIENTS

Serves 4

450 g/1 lb/2½ cups green split peas

4 rindless bacon rashers

1 onion, roughly chopped

2 carrots, sliced

1 celery stick, sliced

2.4 litres/4¼ pints/10½ cups cold water

1 sprig of fresh thyme

2 bay leaves

1 large potato, roughly diced

1 bacon hock

freshly ground black pepper

1 Put the split peas into a bowl, cover with cold water and leave to soak overnight.

2 Cut the bacon into small pieces. In a large saucepan, dry fry the bacon for 4–5 minutes or until crisp. Remove from the pan with a slotted spoon.

3 Add the chopped onion, carrots and celery to the fat in the pan and cook for 3–4 minutes until the onion is softened but not brown. Return the bacon to the pan with the water.

4 Drain the split peas and add to the pan with the thyme, bay leaves, potato and bacon hock. Bring to the boil, reduce the heat, cover and cook gently for 1 hour.

5 Remove the thyme, bay leaves and hock. Process the soup in a blender or food processor until smooth. Return to a clean pan. Cut the meat from the hock, add to the soup and heat through gently. Season with plenty of freshly ground black pepper. Ladle into warm soup bowls and serve.

Lentil, Bacon and Frankfurter Soup

This is a wonderfully hearty German soup, but a lighter version can be made by omitting the frankfurters, if preferred.

INGREDIENTS

Serves 6

225 g/8 oz/1 cup brown lentils
15 ml/1 tbsp sunflower oil
1 onion, finely chopped
1 leek, finely chopped
1 carrot, finely diced
2 celery sticks, chopped
115 g/4 oz piece lean bacon
2 bay leaves
1.5 litres/2½ pints/6¼ cups water
30 ml/2 tbsp chopped fresh parsley, plus
   extra to garnish
225 g/8 oz frankfurters, sliced
salt and freshly ground black pepper

1 Rinse the lentils thoroughly under cold running water, then drain.

2 Heat the oil in a large pan and gently fry the onion for 5 minutes until soft. Add the leek, carrot, celery, bacon and bay leaves.

COOK'S TIP
~
Unlike most pulses, brown lentils do not need to be soaked before cooking.

3 Add the lentils. Pour in the water, then slowly bring to the boil. Skim the surface, then simmer, half-covered, for about 45–50 minutes, or until the lentils are soft.

4 Remove the piece of bacon from the soup and cut into small cubes. Trim off any fat.

5 Return the bacon to the soup with the parsley and sliced frankfurters, and season well with salt and freshly ground black pepper. Simmer for 2–3 minutes, then remove the bay leaves.

6 Transfer to individual soup bowls and serve garnished with chopped parsley.

Pork and Noodle Broth with Prawns

This delicately flavoured soup from Vietnam is quick and easy to make, while tasting really special. The noodles make the soup into a satisfying and wholesome dish.

Serves 4–6

350 g/12 oz pork chops or fillet
225 g/8 oz raw prawn tails or
    cooked prawns
150 g/5 oz thin egg noodles
15 ml/1 tbsp vegetable oil
10 ml/2 tsp sesame oil
4 shallots or 1 medium onion, sliced
15 ml/1 tbsp finely sliced fresh
    root ginger
1 garlic clove, crushed
5 ml/l tsp sugar
1.5 litres/2½ pints/6¼ cups
    chicken stock
2 kaffir lime leaves
45 ml/3 tbsp fish sauce
juice of ½ lime

For the garnish
4 sprigs of fresh coriander
2 spring onions, green parts
    only, chopped

1 If you are using pork chops rather than fillet, remove any fat and the bones. Place the pork in the freezer for 30 minutes to firm, but not freeze it. The cold makes the meat easier to slice thinly. Once sliced, set aside.

2 If using raw prawn tails, peel and devein the prawns.

3 Bring a large saucepan of salted water to the boil and simmer the egg noodles according to the instructions on the packet. Drain and refresh under cold running water. Set the noodles to one side.

4 Preheat a wok. Add the vegetable and sesame oils and heat through. When the oil is hot, add the shallots or onion and stir-fry for 3–4 minutes, until evenly browned. Remove from the wok and set aside.

5 Add the ginger, garlic, sugar and chicken stock to the wok and bring to a simmer. Add the lime leaves, fish sauce and lime juice. Add the pork, then simmer for 15 minutes.

6 Add the prawns and noodles and simmer for 3–4 minutes, or longer if using raw prawns, to ensure that they are cooked.

7 Serve garnished with coriander sprigs and the green parts of the spring onion.

VARIATION
~
This quick and delicious recipe can be made with 200 g/7 oz boneless chicken breast instead of pork fillets.

Three-delicacy Soup

This delicious soup combines the three ingredients of chicken, ham and prawns.

INGREDIENTS

Serves 4

115 g/4 oz chicken breast fillet
115 g/4 oz honey-roast ham
115 g/4 oz peeled prawns
700 ml/1¼ pints/3 cups chicken stock
salt
chopped spring onions, to garnish

1 Thinly slice the chicken breast and ham into small pieces. If the prawns are large, cut them in half lengthways.

2 In a wok or saucepan, bring the stock to a rolling boil and add the chicken, ham and prawns. Bring back to the boil, add salt to taste and simmer for 1 minute.

3 Ladle into individual soup bowls. Serve hot, garnished with chopped spring onions.

COOK'S TIP

Fresh, uncooked prawns impart the best flavour. If these are not available, you can use ready-cooked prawns. They must be added towards the end of cooking, to prevent over-cooking.

Lamb and Cucumber Soup

This is a very simple soup to prepare, but tastes delicious nevertheless.

INGREDIENTS

Serves 4

225 g/8 oz lamb steak
15 ml/1 tbsp light soy sauce
10 ml/2 tsp Chinese rice wine or
   dry sherry
2.5 ml/½ tsp sesame oil
7.5 cm/3 in piece cucumber
750 ml/1¼ pints/3 cups chicken or
   vegetable stock
15 ml/1 tbsp rice vinegar
salt and freshly ground white pepper

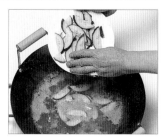

1 Trim off any excess fat from the lamb. Thinly slice the lamb into small pieces. Marinate in the soy sauce, wine or sherry and sesame oil for 25–30 minutes. Discard the marinade.

2 Halve the cucumber piece lengthways (do not peel), then cut into thin slices diagonally.

3 In a wok or saucepan, bring the stock to a rolling boil, add the lamb and stir to separate.

4 Return to the boil, then add the cucumber slices, vinegar and seasoning. Bring back to the boil and serve at once.

Bulgarian Sour Lamb Soup

This traditional sour soup uses lamb, though pork and poultry are popular alternatives.

INGREDIENTS

INGREDIENTS

Serves 4–5

30 ml/2 tbsp oil

450 g/1 1b lean lamb, trimmed and cubed

1 onion, diced

30 ml/2 tbsp plain flour

15 ml/1 tbsp paprika

1 litre/1¾ pints/4 cups hot lamb stock

3 sprigs of fresh parsley

4 spring onions

4 sprigs of fresh dill

25 g/1 oz/scant ¼ cup long-grain rice

2 eggs, beaten

30–45 ml/2–3 tbsp or more vinegar or lemon juice

salt and freshly ground black pepper

For the garnish

25 g/1 oz/2 tbsp butter, melted

5 ml/1 tsp paprika

a little fresh parsley or lovage and dill

1 In a large pan heat the oil and fry the meat until brown. Add the onion and cook until it has softened. Sprinkle in the flour and paprika. Stir well, add the stock and cook for 10 minutes.

2 Tie the parsley, spring onions and dill together with string and add to the large pan with the rice and seasoning. Bring to the boil, then simmer for about 30–40 minutes, or until the lamb is tender.

3 Remove the pan from the heat and stir in the eggs. Add the vinegar or lemon juice. Discard the tied herbs and season to taste.

4 For the garnish, melt the butter in a pan and add the paprika. Ladle the soup into warmed serving bowls. Garnish with the herbs and a little red paprika butter.

Meatball and Pasta Soup

*This soup, which comes from sunny
Sicily, is also substantial enough for
a hearty family supper, whatever
the weather.*

INGREDIENTS

Serves 4

2 x 300 g/11 oz cans condensed
   beef consommé
90 g/3½ oz/¾ cup very thin pasta, such as
   fidelini or spaghettini
chopped fresh flat-leaf parsley, to garnish
grated Parmesan cheese, to serve

For the meatballs
1 very thick slice white bread,
   crusts removed
30 ml/2 tbsp milk
225 g/8 oz/1 cup minced beef
1 garlic clove, crushed
30 ml/2 tbsp grated Parmesan cheese
30–45 ml/2–3 tbsp fresh flat-leaf parsley
   leaves, coarsely chopped
1 egg
a generous pinch of freshly grated nutmeg
salt and freshly ground black pepper

1 Make the meatballs. Break the
bread into a small bowl, add
the milk and set aside to soak.
Meanwhile, put the minced beef,
garlic, Parmesan, parsley and egg
in another large bowl. Grate the
nutmeg liberally over the top and
add salt and pepper to taste.

2 Squeeze the bread with your
hands to remove as much milk
as possible, then add the bread to
the meatball mixture and mix
everything together well with your
hands. Wash your hands, rinse
them under the cold tap, then
form the mixture into tiny balls
about the size of small marbles.

3 Tip both cans of consommé
into a large saucepan, add
water as directed on the labels,
then add an extra can of water.
Season to taste, bring to the boil
and add the meatballs.

4 Break the pasta into small
pieces and add it to the soup.
Bring to the boil, stirring gently.
Simmer, stirring frequently, for
7–8 minutes or according to the
instructions on the packet, until
the pasta is *al dente*. Taste and
adjust the seasoning.

5 Serve hot in warmed bowls,
garnished with chopped
parsley and freshly grated
Parmesan cheese.

Clear Soup with Meatballs

A Chinese-style soup, in which meatballs are combined with lightly cooked vegetables in a tasty stock.

INGREDIENTS

Serves 8

4–6 Chinese mushrooms, soaked in warm
  water for 30 minutes
30 ml/2 tbsp groundnut oil
1 large onion, finely chopped
2 garlic cloves, finely crushed
1 cm/½ in piece fresh root ginger, bruised
2 litres/3½ pints/9 cups beef or chicken
  stock, including soaking liquid from the
  mushrooms
30 ml/2 tbsp soy sauce
115 g/4 oz curly kale, spinach or Chinese
  leaves, shredded

For the meatballs
175 g/6 oz/¾ cup finely minced beef
1 small onion, finely chopped
1–2 garlic cloves, crushed
15 ml/1 tbsp cornflour
a little egg white, lightly beaten
salt and freshly ground black pepper

1 First prepare the meatballs. Mix the beef with the onion, garlic, cornflour and seasoning in a food processor and then bind with sufficient egg white to make a firm mixture. With wet hands, roll into tiny, bite-size balls and set aside.

2 Drain the mushrooms. Reserve the soaking liquid. Trim off and discard the stalks. Slice the caps finely and set aside.

3 Heat a wok or large saucepan and add the oil. Fry the onion, garlic and ginger to bring out the flavour, but do not allow to brown.

4 When the onion is soft, pour in the stock. Bring to the boil, then stir in the soy sauce and mushroom slices and simmer for 10 minutes. Add the meatballs and cook for 10 minutes.

5 Just before serving, remove the ginger. Stir in the shredded curly kale, spinach or Chinese leaves. Heat through for 1 minute only – no longer or the leaves will be overcooked. Serve the soup immediately.

Pork and Vegetable Soup

The unusual ingredients in this interesting Japanese soup are available from specialist food stores.

Serves 4

50 g/2 oz gobo (optional)

5 ml/1 tsp rice vinegar

½ black konnyaku (about 115 g/4 oz)

10 ml/2 tsp oil

200 g/7 oz pork belly, cut into thin 3–4 cm/1¼–1½ in long strips

115 g/4 oz mooli, peeled and thinly sliced

50 g/2 oz carrot, thinly sliced

1 medium potato, thinly sliced

4 shiitake mushrooms, stems removed and thinly sliced

800 ml/scant 1½ pints/3½ cups kombu and bonito stock or instant dashi

15 ml/1 tbsp sake or dry white wine

45 ml/3 tbsp red or white miso paste

For the garnish

2 spring onions, thinly sliced

seven spice flavour (shichimi)

1 Scrub the skin off the gobo, if using, with a vegetable brush. Slice the vegetable into fine shavings. Soak the prepared gobo for 5 minutes in plenty of water with the vinegar added to remove any bitter taste, then drain.

2 Put the piece of konnyaku in a small pan and add enough water just to cover it. Bring to the boil over a moderate heat, then drain and allow to cool. This removes any bitter taste.

3 Using your hands, tear the konnyaku into 2 cm/¾ in lumps. Do not use a knife as a smooth cut surface will not absorb any flavour.

4 Heat the oil in a saucepan and quickly stir-fry the pork. Add the gobo, mooli, carrot, potato, shiitake mushrooms and konnyaku, then stir-fry for 1 minute. Pour in the stock and sake or wine.

5 Bring the soup to the boil, then skim it and simmer for 10 minutes, until the vegetables have softened.

6 Ladle a little of the soup into a small bowl and dissolve the miso paste in it. Pour back into the saucepan and return to the boil. Do not continue to boil or the flavour will be lost. Remove from the heat, then pour into individual serving bowls. Sprinkle with the spring onions and seven spice flavour (shichimi) and serve immediately.

Tomato and Beef Soup

Fresh tomatoes and spring onions give this light beef broth a superb flavour and appearance.

INGREDIENTS

Serves 4

75 g/3 oz rump steak, trimmed of fat
900 ml/1½ pints/3¾ cups beef stock
30 ml/2 tbsp tomato purée
6 tomatoes, halved, seeded and chopped
10 ml/2 tsp caster sugar
15 ml/1 tbsp cornflour
15 ml/l tbsp cold water
1 egg white
2.5 ml/½ tsp sesame oil
2 spring onions, finely shredded
salt and freshly ground black pepper

3 Mix the cornflour to a paste with the cold water. Add the paste to the soup, stirring constantly until it thickens slightly but does not become lumpy. Lightly beat the egg white in a cup.

4 Pour the egg white into the soup in a steady stream, stirring all the time. As soon as the egg white changes colour, add salt and pepper, stir the soup and pour it into heated bowls. Drizzle a few drops of sesame oil on each portion, sprinkle with the spring onions and serve.

1 Cut the beef into thin strips and place it in a saucepan. Pour over boiling water to cover. Cook for 2 minutes, then drain thoroughly and set aside.

2 Bring the stock to the boil in a clean pan. Stir in the tomato purée, then the tomatoes and sugar. Add the beef, allow the stock to boil again, then lower the heat and simmer for 2 minutes.

Beef Chilli Soup

This is a hearty dish based on a traditional chilli recipe. It is ideal served with fresh, crusty bread as a warming start to any meal.

INGREDIENTS

Serves 4

15 ml/1 tbsp oil

1 onion, chopped

175 g/6 oz/³⁄₄ cup minced beef

2 garlic cloves, chopped

1 fresh red chilli, sliced

25 g/1 oz/¹⁄₄ cup plain flour

400 g/14 oz can chopped tomatoes

600 ml/1 pint/2¹⁄₂ cups beef stock

225 g/8 oz/2 cups canned kidney beans, drained

30 ml/2 tbsp chopped fresh parsley

salt and freshly ground black pepper

crusty bread, to serve

1 Heat the oil in a large saucepan. Fry the onion and minced beef for 5 minutes until brown and sealed.

2 Add the garlic, chilli and flour. Cook for 1 minute. Add the tomatoes and pour in the stock. Bring to the boil.

3 Stir in the kidney beans and add salt and pepper to taste. Cook for 20 minutes.

4 Add the chopped parsley, reserving a little to garnish the finished dish. Pour the soup into warm bowls, sprinkle with the reserved parsley and serve with crusty bread.

COOK'S TIP

For a milder flavour, remove the seeds from the chilli after slicing.

ONE-POT-MEAL
SOUPS

~

V

Tuscan Bean Soup

There are many versions of this wonderful soup. This one uses cannellini beans, leeks, cabbage and good olive oil – and tastes even better when it is reheated.

INGREDIENTS

Serves 4

45 ml/3 tbsp extra-virgin olive oil
1 onion, roughly chopped
2 leeks, roughly chopped
1 large potato, diced
2 garlic cloves, finely chopped
1.2 litres/2 pints/5 cups vegetable stock
400 g/14 oz can cannellini beans, drained
  and liquid reserved
175 g/6 oz Savoy cabbage, shredded
45 ml/3 tbsp chopped fresh flat-leaf parsley
30 ml/2 tbsp chopped fresh oregano
75 g/3 oz/1 cup Parmesan cheese, shaved
salt and freshly ground black pepper

For the garlic toasts
30–45 ml/2–3 tbsp extra-virgin olive oil
6 thick slices country bread
1 garlic clove, peeled and bruised

1 Heat the oil in a large saucepan and gently cook the onion, leeks, potato and garlic for 4–5 minutes until they are just beginning to soften.

2 Pour on the stock and the liquid from the beans. Cover and simmer for 15 minutes.

3 Stir in the cabbage, beans and half the herbs, season and cook for a further 10 minutes. Spoon about one-third of the soup into a food processor or blender and process until fairly smooth. Return to the soup in the pan, adjust the seasoning and heat through for 5 minutes.

4 Make the garlic toasts. Drizzle a little oil over the slices of bread, then rub both sides of each slice with the garlic. Toast until browned on both sides. Ladle the soup into bowls. Sprinkle with the remaining herbs and the Parmesan shavings. Add a drizzle of olive oil and serve with the hot garlic toasts.

Farmhouse Soup

Root vegetables form the base of this chunky, minestrone-style, main-meal soup. You can vary the vegetables according to what you have to hand.

INGREDIENTS

Serves 4

30 ml/2 tbsp olive oil

1 onion, roughly chopped

3 carrots, cut into large chunks

175–200 g/6–7 oz turnips, cut into large chunks

about 175 g/6 oz swede, cut into large chunks

400 g/14 oz can chopped Italian tomatoes

15 ml/1 tbsp tomato purée

5 ml/1 tsp dried mixed herbs

5 ml/1 tsp dried oregano

50 g/2 oz/^{1}/$_2$ cup dried peppers, finely sliced (optional)

1.5 litres/2^1/$_2$ pints/6^1/$_4$ cups vegetable stock or water

50 g/2 oz/^{1}/$_2$ cup small macaroni or conchiglie

400 g/14 oz can red kidney beans, rinsed and drained

30 ml/2 tbsp chopped fresh flat-leaf parsley

salt and freshly ground black pepper

grated Parmesan cheese, to serve

1 Heat the oil in a large saucepan, add the onion and cook over a low heat for about 5 minutes until softened. Add the fresh vegetables, canned tomatoes, tomato purée, dried herbs and dried peppers, if using. Stir in salt and pepper to taste.

2 Pour in the stock or water and bring to the boil. Stir well, cover, lower the heat and simmer for 30 minutes, stirring occasionally.

3 Add the pasta and bring to the boil, stirring. Lower the heat and simmer, uncovered, for about 5 minutes or according to the instructions on the packet until the pasta is just *al dente*. Stir frequently during the cooking.

4 Stir in the beans. Heat through for 2–3 minutes, then remove from the heat and stir in the parsley. Taste and adjust the seasoning. Serve hot in warmed soup bowls and hand round the grated Parmesan separately.

COOK'S TIP

Packets of dried Italian peppers are sold in many supermarkets and in delicatessens. They are piquant and firm with a "meaty" bite to them, which makes them ideal for adding substance to vegetarian soups.

V

Provençale Vegetable Soup

*This satisfying soup captures all the
flavours of summer in Provence.
The basil and garlic purée, pistou,
gives it extra colour and a wonderful
aroma – so don't leave it out.*

INGREDIENTS

Serves 6–8

275 g/10 oz/1½ cups shelled fresh broad
    beans or 175 g/6 oz/¾ cup dried haricot
    beans, soaked overnight
2.5 ml/½ tsp dried herbes de Provence
2 garlic cloves, finely chopped
15 ml/1 tbsp olive oil
1 onion, finely chopped
1 large leek, finely sliced
1 celery stick, finely sliced
2 carrots, finely diced
2 small potatoes, finely diced
115 g/4 oz French beans
1.2 litres/2 pints/5 cups water
2 small courgettes, finely chopped
3 medium tomatoes, peeled, seeded and
    finely chopped
115 g/4 oz/l cup shelled garden peas, fresh
    or frozen
a handful of spinach leaves, cut into
    thin ribbons
salt and freshly ground black pepper
sprigs of fresh basil, to garnish

For the pistou

1 or 2 garlic cloves, finely chopped
15 g/½ oz/½ cup (packed) basil leaves
60 ml/4 tbsp grated Parmesan cheese
60 ml/4 tbsp extra-virgin olive oil

1 To make the pistou, put the
  garlic, basil and Parmesan
cheese in a food processor and
process until smooth, scraping
down the sides once. With the
machine running, slowly add the
olive oil through the feed tube.
Alternatively, pound the garlic,
basil and cheese in a mortar and
pestle and stir in the oil.

2 To make the soup, if using
  dried haricot beans, drain
them, place in a saucepan and
cover with water. Boil vigorously
for 10 minutes and drain.

3 Place the par-boiled beans,
  or fresh beans if using, in a
saucepan with the herbes de
Provence and one of the garlic
cloves. Add water to cover by
2.5 cm/l in. Bring to the boil,
reduce the heat and simmer over
a medium-low heat until tender,
about 10 minutes for fresh beans
or 1 hour for dried beans. Set aside
in the cooking liquid.

4 Heat the oil in a large
  saucepan or flameproof
casserole. Add the onion and leek
and cook for 5 minutes, stirring
occasionally, until they are
beginning to soften.

5 Add the celery, carrots and
  the remaining garlic clove and
cook, covered, for 10 minutes,
stirring occasionally.

6 Add the potatoes, French
  beans and water, then season
lightly with salt and pepper. Bring
to the boil, skimming any foam
that rises to the surface, then
reduce the heat, cover and simmer
gently for 10 minutes.

7 Add the courgettes, tomatoes
  and peas, together with the
reserved beans and their cooking
liquid, and simmer for about
25–30 minutes until all the
vegetables are tender. Add the
spinach and simmer for 5 minutes.
Season the soup and swirl a
spoonful of pistou into each bowl.
Garnish with basil and serve.

COOK'S TIP

Both the pistou and the soup can
be made 1 or 2 days in advance
and chilled. To serve, reheat
gently, stirring occasionally.

V

Chunky Bean and Vegetable Soup

A substantial soup, not unlike minestrone, using a selection of vegetables, with cannellini beans for extra protein and fibre. Serve with a hunk of wholegrain bread.

INGREDIENTS

Serves 4

30 ml/2 tbsp olive oil

2 celery sticks, chopped

2 leeks, sliced

3 carrots, sliced

2 garlic cloves, crushed

400 g/14 oz can chopped tomatoes with basil

1.2 litres/2 pints/5 cups vegetable stock

400 g/14 oz can cannellini beans (or mixed pulses), drained

15 ml/1 tbsp pesto sauce

salt and freshly ground black pepper

Parmesan cheese shavings, to serve

1 Heat the olive oil in a large saucepan. Add the celery, leeks, carrots and garlic and cook gently for about 5 minutes until they have softened.

2 Stir in the tomatoes and stock. Bring to the boil, then cover and cook gently for 15 minutes.

3 Stir in the beans and pesto, with salt and pepper to taste. Heat through for a further 5 minutes. Serve in heated bowls, sprinkled with shavings of Parmesan cheese.

COOK'S TIP

Extra vegetables can be added to the soup to make it even more substantial. For example, add some thinly sliced courgettes or finely shredded cabbage for the last 5 minutes of the cooking time. Or, stir in some small wholewheat pasta shapes, if liked. Add them at the same time as the tomatoes, as they will take 10–15 minutes to cook.

Caribbean Vegetable Soup

This vegetable soup is refreshing and filling, and a good choice for a main lunch dish.

INGREDIENTS

Serves 4

25 g/1 oz/2 tbsp butter or margarine

1 onion, chopped

1 garlic clove, crushed

2 carrots, sliced

1.5 litres/2½ pints/6¼ cups vegetable stock

2 bay leaves

2 sprigs of fresh thyme

1 celery stick, finely chopped

2 green bananas, peeled and cut into 4 pieces

175 g/6 oz white yam or eddoe, peeled and cubed

25 g/1 oz/2 tbsp red lentils

1 christophene, peeled and chopped

25 g/1 oz/2 tbsp macaroni (optional)

salt and freshly ground black pepper

chopped spring onions, to garnish

COOK'S TIP

Use other root vegetables or potatoes if yam or eddoes are not available. Add more stock if you want a thinner soup.

1 Melt the butter or margarine and fry the onion, garlic and carrots for a few minutes, stirring occasionally, until beginning to soften. Add the stock, bay leaves and thyme and bring to the boil.

2 Add the celery, green bananas, white yam or eddoe, lentils, christophene and macaroni, if using. Season and simmer for 25 minutes or until all the vegetables are cooked. Serve garnished with chopped spring onions.

Chunky Pasta Soup

Serve this hearty, main-meal soup with tasty, pesto-topped French bread croûtons.

INGREDIENTS

Serves 4

115 g/4 oz/½ cup dried beans (a mixture of red kidney and haricot beans), soaked overnight

1.2 litres/2 pints/5 cups water

15 ml/1 tbsp oil

1 onion, chopped

2 celery sticks, finely sliced

2–3 garlic cloves, crushed

2 leeks, finely sliced

1 vegetable stock cube

400 g/14 oz can or jar pimientos

45–60 ml/3–4 tbsp tomato purée

115 g/4 oz pasta shapes

4 slices French bread

15 ml/1 tbsp pesto sauce

115 g/4 oz/l cup baby sweetcorn, halved

50 g/2 oz each broccoli and cauliflower florets

a few drops of Tabasco sauce

salt and freshly ground black pepper

1 Drain the beans and place in a large pan with the water. Bring to the boil and simmer for about 1 hour, or until nearly tender.

2 When the beans are almost ready, heat the oil in a large pan and fry the vegetables for 2 minutes. Add the stock cube and the beans with about 600 ml/1 pint/ 2½ cups of their liquid. Cover and simmer for 10 minutes.

3 Meanwhile, purée the pimientos with a little of their liquid and add to the pan. Stir in the tomato purée and pasta and cook for 15 minutes. Preheat the oven to 200°C/400°F/Gas 6.

4 Meanwhile, make the pesto croûtons. Spread the French bread with the pesto sauce and bake for 10 minutes or until crisp.

5 When the pasta is just cooked, add the sweetcorn, broccoli and cauliflower florets, Tabasco sauce and seasoning to taste. Heat through for 2–3 minutes and serve at once with the pesto croûtons.

Japanese Crushed Tofu Soup

The main ingredient for this soup is crushed tofu, which is both nutritious and satisfying.

INGREDIENTS

Serves 4

150 g/5 oz fresh tofu, weighed without
    water
2 dried shiitake mushrooms
50 g/2 oz gobo
5 ml/1 tsp rice vinegar
½ black or white konnyaku (about 115 g/
    4 oz)
30 ml/2 tbsp sesame oil
115 g/4 oz mooli, finely sliced
50 g/2 oz carrot, finely sliced
750 ml/1¼ pints/3 cups kombu and
    bonito stock or instant dashi
a pinch of salt
30 ml/2 tbsp sake or dry white wine
7.5 ml/1½ tsp mirin
45 ml/3 tbsp white or red miso paste
a dash of soy sauce
6 mangetouts, trimmed, boiled and finely
    sliced, to garnish

1 Crush the tofu roughly by hand until it resembles lumpy scrambled egg in texture – do not crush it too finely.

2 Wrap the tofu in a clean tea towel and put it in a sieve, then pour over plenty of boiling water. Leave the tofu to drain thoroughly for 10 minutes.

3 Soak the dried shiitake mushrooms in tepid water for 20 minutes, then drain them. Remove their stems and cut the caps into 4–6 pieces.

4 Use a vegetable brush to scrub the skin off the gobo and slice it into thin shavings. Soak the shavings for 5 minutes in plenty of cold water with the vinegar added to remove any bitter taste. Drain.

5 Put the konnyaku in a small saucepan and cover with water. Bring to the boil, then drain and cool. Tear the konnyaku into 2 cm/¾ in lumps: do not use a knife, as smooth cuts will prevent it from absorbing flavour.

6 Heat the sesame oil in a deep saucepan. Add all the shiitake mushrooms, gobo, mooli, carrot and konnyaku. Stir-fry for 1 minute, then add the tofu and stir well.

7 Pour in the stock/dashi and add the salt, sake or wine and mirin. Bring to the boil. Skim the broth and simmer it for 5 minutes.

8 In a small bowl, dissolve the miso paste in a little of the soup, then return it to the pan. Simmer the soup gently for 10 minutes, until the vegetables are soft. Add the soy sauce, then remove from the heat. Serve immediately in 4 bowls, garnished with the mangetouts.

V

Genoese Minestrone

In Genoa, they often make minestrone like this, with pesto stirred in towards the end of cooking. It is packed full of vegetables and has a strong, heady flavour, making it an excellent vegetarian supper dish when served with bread. There is Parmesan cheese in the pesto, so there is no need to serve any extra with the soup.

INGREDIENTS

Serves 4–6

45 ml/3 tbsp olive oil
1 onion, finely chopped
2 celery sticks, finely chopped
1 large carrot, finely chopped
150 g/5 oz French beans, cut into 5 cm/
   2 in pieces
1 courgette, finely sliced
1 potato, cut into 1 cm/1/2 in cubes
1/4 Savoy cabbage, shredded
1 small aubergine, cut into 1 cm/1/2 in
   cubes
200 g/7 oz can cannellini beans, drained
   and rinsed
2 Italian plum tomatoes, chopped
1.2 litres/2 pints/5 cups vegetable stock
90 g/31/2 oz spaghetti or vermicelli
salt and freshly ground black pepper

For the pesto
about 20 fresh basil leaves
1 garlic clove
10 ml/2 tsp pine nuts
15 ml/1 tbsp freshly grated Parmesan
   cheese
15 ml/1 tbsp freshly grated pecorino
   cheese
30 ml/2 tbsp olive oil

1 Heat the oil in a large saucepan, add the chopped onion, celery and carrot, and cook over a low heat, stirring frequently, for 5–7 minutes.

2 Mix in the French beans, courgette, potato and Savoy cabbage. Stir-fry over a medium heat for about 3 minutes. Add the aubergine, cannellini beans and plum tomatoes and stir-fry for 2–3 minutes.

3 Pour in the stock with salt and pepper to taste. Bring to the boil. Stir well, cover and lower the heat. Simmer for 40 minutes, stirring occasionally.

4 Meanwhile, process all the pesto ingredients in a food processor until the mixture forms a smooth sauce, adding 15–45 ml/ 1–3 tbsp water through the feeder tube if the sauce seems too thick.

5 Break the pasta into small pieces and add it to the soup. Simmer, stirring frequently, for 5 minutes. Add the pesto sauce and stir it in well, then simmer for 2–3 minutes more, or until the pasta is *al dente*. Check the seasoning and serve hot, in warmed soup plates or bowls.

Summer Minestrone

V

This brightly coloured, fresh-tasting soup makes the most of delicious summer vegetables.

INGREDIENTS

Serves 4

45 ml/3 tbsp olive oil

1 large onion, finely chopped

15ml/1 tbsp sun-dried tomato purée

450 g/1 lb ripe Italian plum tomatoes, peeled and finely chopped

225 g/8 oz green courgettes, trimmed and roughly chopped

225 g/8 oz yellow courgettes, trimmed and roughly chopped

3 waxy new potatoes, diced

2 garlic cloves, crushed

about 1.2 litres/2 pints/5 cups vegetable stock or water

60 ml/4 tbsp shredded fresh basil

50 g/2 oz/²⁄₃ cup grated Parmesan cheese

salt and freshly ground black pepper

1 Heat the oil in a large saucepan, add the onion and cook gently for about 5 minutes, stirring constantly, until softened.

2 Stir in the sun-dried tomato purée, chopped tomatoes, courgettes, diced potatoes and garlic. Mix well and cook gently for 10 minutes, uncovered, shaking the pan frequently to stop the vegetables sticking to the base.

3 Pour in the stock or water. Bring to the boil, lower the heat, half-cover the pan and simmer gently for 15 minutes or until the vegetables are just tender. Add more stock if necessary.

4 Remove the pan from the heat and stir in the basil and half the cheese. Taste and adjust the seasoning. Serve hot, sprinkled with the remaining cheese.

Seafood Laksa

For a delicious meal, serve creamy rice noodles in a spicy coconut-flavoured soup, topped with seafood. There is a fair amount of work involved in the preparation, but you can make the soup base in advance.

INGREDIENTS

Serves 4

4 fresh red chillies, seeded and roughly
    chopped
1 onion, roughly chopped
1 piece blacan, the size of a stock cube
1 lemon grass stalk, chopped
1 small piece fresh root ginger, peeled and
    roughly chopped
6 macadamia nuts or almonds
60 ml/4 tbsp vegetable oil
5 ml/1 tsp paprika
5 ml/1 tsp ground turmeric
475 ml/16 fl oz/2 cups fish stock
600 ml/1 pint/2½ cups coconut milk
a dash of fish sauce, to taste
12 king prawns, peeled and deveined
8 scallops
225 g/8 oz prepared squid, cut into rings
350 g/12 oz rice vermicelli or rice noodles,
    soaked in warm water until soft
salt and freshly ground black pepper
lime halves, to serve

For the garnish
¼ cucumber, cut into matchsticks
2 fresh red chillies, seeded and finely
    sliced
30 ml/2 tbsp mint leaves
30 ml/2 tbsp fried shallots or onions

1 In a blender or food processor, process the chillies, onion, blacan, lemon grass, ginger and nuts until smooth in texture.

2 Heat 45 ml/3 tbsp of the oil in a large saucepan. Add the chilli paste and fry for 6 minutes. Stir in the paprika and turmeric and fry for about 2 minutes more.

3 Add the stock and the coconut milk to the pan. Bring to the boil, then simmer gently for 15–20 minutes. Season with fish sauce.

4 Season the seafood with salt and pepper. Fry quickly in the remaining oil for 2–3 minutes until cooked.

5 Add the noodles to the soup and heat through. Divide among individual serving bowls. Place the fried seafood on top, then garnish with the cucumber, chillies, mint and fried shallots or onions. Serve with the limes.

Clam and Pasta Soup

This soup is a variation of the pasta dish spaghetti alle vongole, *using store-cupboard ingredients. Serve it with hot focaccia or ciabatta for an informal supper with friends.*

Serves 4

30 ml/2 tbsp olive oil

1 large onion, finely chopped

2 garlic cloves, crushed

400 g/14 oz can chopped tomatoes

15 ml/1 tbsp sun-dried tomato purée

5 ml/1 tsp granulated sugar

5 ml/1 tsp dried mixed herbs

about 750 ml/1¼ pints/3 cups fish or
    vegetable stock

150 ml/¼ pint/⅔ cup red wine

50 g/2 oz/½ cup small pasta shapes

150 g/5 oz jar or can clams in natural juice

30 ml/2 tbsp finely chopped fresh flat-leaf
    parsley, plus a few whole leaves
    to garnish

salt and freshly ground black pepper

1 Heat the oil in a large saucepan. Cook the onion gently for 5 minutes, stirring frequently, until softened.

2 Add the garlic, tomatoes, tomato purée, sugar, herbs, stock and wine, with salt and pepper to taste. Bring to the boil. Lower the heat, half-cover the pan and simmer for 10 minutes, stirring occasionally.

3 Add the pasta and continue simmering, uncovered, for about 10 minutes or until *al dente*. Stir occasionally to prevent the pasta shapes sticking together.

4 Add the clams and their juice to the soup and heat through for 3–4 minutes, adding more stock if required. Do not allow it to boil, or the clams will become tough. Remove from the heat, stir in the chopped parsley and adjust the seasoning. Serve hot, sprinkled with coarsely ground black pepper and parsley leaves.

Prawn Creole

Raw prawns are combined with chopped fresh vegetables and cayenne pepper to make this tasty soup.

INGREDIENTS

Serves 4

675 g/1½ lb raw prawns in the shell, with
   heads, if available
475 ml/16 fl oz/2 cups water
45 ml/3 tbsp olive or vegetable oil
175 g/6 oz/1½ cups onions, very finely
   chopped
75 g/3 oz/½ cup celery, very finely chopped
75 g/3 oz/½ cup green pepper, very finely
   chopped
25 g/1 oz/½ cup chopped fresh parsley
1 garlic clove, crushed
15 ml/1 tbsp Worcestershire sauce
1.5 ml/¼ tsp cayenne pepper
120 ml/4 fl oz/½ cup dry white wine
50 g/2 oz/1 cup chopped peeled plum
   tomatoes
5 ml/1 tsp salt
1 bay leaf
5ml/1 tsp sugar
fresh parsley, to garnish
boiled rice, to serve

1 Peel and devein the prawns, reserving the heads and shells. Keep the prawns in a covered bowl in the refrigerator while you make the sauce.

2 Put the prawn heads and shells in a pan with the water. Bring to the boil and simmer for 15 minutes. Strain and reserve 350 ml/12 fl oz/1½ cups of the stock.

3 Heat the oil in a heavy saucepan. Add the onions and cook over a low heat for 8–10 minutes until softened. Add the celery and green pepper and cook for 5 minutes further. Stir in the parsley, garlic, Worcestershire sauce and cayenne. Cook for another 5 minutes.

4 Raise the heat to medium. Stir in the wine and simmer for 3–4 minutes. Add the tomatoes, reserved prawn stock, salt, bay leaf and sugar and bring to the boil. Stir well, then reduce the heat to low and simmer for about 30 minutes until the tomatoes have fallen apart and the sauce has reduced slightly. Remove from the heat and cool slightly.

5 Discard the bay leaf. Pour the sauce into a food processor or blender and purée until quite smooth. Taste and adjust the seasoning as necessary.

6 Return the tomato sauce to the pan and bring to the boil. Add the prawns and simmer for 4–5 minutes until they turn pink. Ladle into individual soup bowls, garnish with fresh parsley and serve with rice.

Creamy Fish Chowder

A traditional soup that never fails to please, whether it is made with milk or more luxuriously, with a generous quantity of cream.

INGREDIENTS

Serves 4

3 thick-cut bacon rashers
1 large onion
675 g/1½ potatoes
1 litre/1¾ pints/4 cups fish stock
450 g/1 lb skinless haddock, cut into
  2.5 cm/1 in cubes
30 ml/2 tbsp chopped fresh parsley
15 ml/1 tbsp snipped fresh chives
300 ml/½ pint/1¼ cups whipping cream
  or whole milk
salt and freshly ground black pepper

1 Remove the rind from the bacon and discard it; cut the bacon into small pieces. Chop the onion and cut the potatoes into 2 cm/¾ in cubes.

2 Fry the bacon in a deep saucepan until the fat is rendered. Add the onion and potatoes and cook over low heat, without browning, for about 10 minutes. Season to taste.

5 Stir the cream or milk into the chowder and reheat gently, but do not bring to the boil. Season to taste and serve immediately.

3 Pour off excess bacon fat from the pan. Add the fish stock to the pan and bring to a boil. Simmer until the vegetables are tender, about 15–20 minutes.

4 Stir in the cubes of fish, the parsley and chives. Simmer until the fish is just cooked, 3–4 minutes.

VARIATION

Cod fillets would be equally good in this chowder, or try smoked fillets for a stronger taste.

Bouillabaisse

Perhaps the most famous of all Mediterranean fish soups, this recipe, originating from Marseilles in the south of France, is a rich and colourful mixture of fish and shellfish, flavoured with tomatoes, saffron and orange.

INGREDIENTS

Serves 4–6

1.5 kg/3–3½ lb mixed fish and raw
    shellfish, such as red mullet, John Dory,
    monkfish, red snapper, whiting, large
    raw prawns and clams
225 g/8 oz well-flavoured tomatoes
a pinch of saffron strands
90 ml/6 tbsp olive oil
1 onion, sliced
1 leek, sliced
1 celery stick, sliced
2 garlic cloves, crushed
1 bouquet garni
1 strip orange rind
2.5 ml/½ tsp fennel seeds
15 ml/1 tbsp tomato purée
10 ml/2 tsp Pernod
salt and freshly ground black pepper
4–6 thick slices French bread and
    45 ml/3 tbsp chopped fresh parsley,
    to serve

COOK'S TIP

Saffron comes from the orange and red stigmas of a type of crocus, which must be harvested by hand and are therefore extremely expensive – the highest-priced spice in the world. However, its flavour is unique and cannot be replaced by any other spice. It is an essential ingredient in traditional bouillabaisse and should not be omitted.

1 Remove the heads, tails and fins from the fish and set the fish aside. Put the trimmings in a large pan with 1.2 litres/2 pints/ 5 cups water. Bring to the boil and simmer for 15 minutes. Strain and reserve the liquid.

2 Cut the fish into large chunks. Leave the shellfish in their shells. Scald the tomatoes, then drain and refresh in cold water. Peel them and chop roughly. Soak the saffron in 15–30 ml/1–2 tbsp hot water.

3 Heat the oil in a large pan, add the onion, leek and celery and cook until softened. Add the garlic, bouquet garni, orange rind, fennel seeds and chopped tomatoes, then stir in the saffron and its soaking liquid and the reserved fish stock. Season with salt and pepper, then bring to the boil and simmer for 30–40 minutes.

4 Add the shellfish and boil for about 6 minutes. Add the fish and cook for 6–8 minutes more, until it flakes easily.

5 Using a slotted spoon, transfer the fish to a warmed serving platter. Keep the liquid boiling, to allow the oil to emulsify with the broth. Add the tomato purée and Pernod, then check the seasoning.

6 Ladle into warm bowls, scatter with chopped parsley and serve with French bread.

Provençale Fish Soup with Pasta

This colourful soup has all the flavours of the Mediterranean. Serve it as a main course for a deliciously filling lunch.

INGREDIENTS

Serves 4

30 ml/2 tbsp olive oil
1 onion, sliced
1 garlic clove, crushed
1 leek, sliced
1 litre/1¾ pints/4 cups water
225 g/8 oz canned chopped tomatoes
a pinch of Mediterranean herbs
1.5 ml/¼ tsp saffron strands (optional)
115 g/4 oz small pasta
about 8 live mussels in the shell
450 g/1 lb white fish, such as cod, plaice or
    monkfish, filleted and skinned
salt and freshly ground black pepper

For the rouille
2 garlic cloves, crushed
1 canned pimiento, drained and chopped
15 ml/1 tbsp fresh white breadcrumbs
60 ml/4 tbsp mayonnaise
toasted French bread, to serve

1 Heat the oil in a large saucepan and add the onion, garlic and leek. Cover and cook gently for 5 minutes, stirring occasionally, until the vegetables are soft.

2 Add the water, tomatoes, herbs, saffron, if using, and pasta. Season and cook for 15–20 minutes.

3 Scrub the mussels and pull off the "beards". Discard any that do not close when sharply tapped.

4 Cut the fish into bite-size chunks and add to the soup, placing the mussels on top. Simmer for 5–10 minutes until the mussels open and the fish is cooked. Discard any unopened mussels.

5 To make the rouille, pound together the garlic, canned pimiento and breadcrumbs in a pestle and mortar (or in a blender or food processor). Stir in the mayonnaise and season well.

6 Spread the toasted French bread with the rouille and serve with the soup.

Fisherman's Soup

There is something truly delicious about the combined flavours of bacon and fish.

INGREDIENTS

Serves 4

6 streaky bacon rashers, cut into strips
15 g/½ oz/1 tbsp butter
1 large onion, chopped
1 garlic clove, finely chopped
30 ml/2 tbsp chopped fresh parsley
5 ml/1 tsp fresh thyme leaves or 2.5 ml/
   ½ tsp dried thyme
450 g/1 lb tomatoes, peeled, seeded
   and chopped
150 ml/¼ pint/⅔ cup dry vermouth or
   white wine
450 ml/¾ pint/scant 2 cups fish stock
300 g/11 oz potatoes, diced
675–900 g/1½–2 lb skinless white fish
   fillets, cut into large chunks
salt and freshly ground black pepper
fresh flat-leaf parsley, to garnish

1 Fry the bacon in a large saucepan over moderate heat until lightly browned but not crisp. Remove from the pan and drain on kitchen paper.

2 Add the butter to the pan and cook the onion, stirring occasionally, for 3–5 minutes until soft. Add the garlic and herbs and continue cooking for 1 minute, stirring. Add the tomatoes, vermouth or wine and stock and bring to the boil.

3 Reduce the heat, cover and simmer the stew for 15 minutes. Add the potatoes, cover again and simmer for a further 10–12 minutes or until the potatoes are almost tender.

COOK'S TIP

In winter, when fresh tomatoes are lacking in flavour, you can substitute canned chopped tomatoes. The soup will taste slightly different but will still be successful.

4 Add the chunks of fish and the bacon strips. Simmer gently, uncovered, for 5 minutes or until the fish is just cooked and the potatoes are tender. Adjust the seasoning, garnish with flat-leaf parsley and serve.

Sweetcorn Chowder with Conchigliette

Sweetcorn kernels combine with smoked turkey and pasta to make this satisfying and filling one-pot meal, perfect for a hungry family or for guests.

INGREDIENTS

Serves 6–8

1 small green pepper
450 g/1 lb potatoes, diced
350 g/12 oz/2 cups canned or frozen
   sweetcorn kernels
1 onion, chopped
1 celery stick, chopped
1 bouquet garni
600 ml/1 pint/2½ cups chicken stock
300 ml/½ pint/1¼ cups skimmed milk
50 g/2 oz conchigliette
oil, for frying
150 g/5 oz smoked turkey rashers, diced
salt and freshly ground black pepper
breadsticks, to serve

3 Add the milk and salt and pepper. Process half of the soup in a food processor or blender and return to the pan with the pasta. Simmer for 10 minutes or until the pasta is *al dente*.

4 Heat the oil in a non-stick frying pan and fry the turkey rashers quickly for 2–3 minutes. Stir into the soup. Serve the soup with breadsticks.

1 Seed the green pepper and cut into dice. Cover with boiling water and leave to stand for 2 minutes. Drain and rinse.

2 Put the potatoes into a saucepan with the sweetcorn, onion, celery, diced pepper, bouquet garni and stock. Bring to the boil, cover and simmer for 20 minutes until tender.

Thai Chicken and Noodle Soup

This makes full use of the characteristic Thai flavours of garlic, coconut, lemon, peanut butter, fresh coriander and chilli.

INGREDIENTS

Serves 4

15 ml/1 tbsp vegetable oil

1 garlic clove, finely chopped

2 skinless, boneless chicken breasts
   (175 g/6 oz each) chopped

2.5 ml/¹⁄₂ tsp ground turmeric

1.5 ml/¹⁄₄ tsp hot chilli powder

75 g/3 oz/¹⁄₂ cup creamed coconut

900 ml/1¹⁄₂ pints/3³⁄₄ cups hot chicken
   stock

30 ml/2 tbsp lemon or lime juice

30 ml/2 tbsp crunchy peanut butter

50 g/2 oz/1 cup thread egg noodles,
   broken into small pieces

15ml/1 tbsp chopped spring onions

15ml/1 tbsp chopped fresh coriander

salt and freshly ground black pepper

desiccated coconut and finely chopped
   fresh red chilli, to garnish

1 Heat the oil in a large pan and fry the garlic for 1 minute until lightly golden. Add the chicken and spices. Stir-fry for 3–4 minutes.

2 Crumble the creamed coconut into the hot chicken stock and stir until dissolved. Pour on to the chicken breasts and add the lemon or lime juice, peanut butter and thread egg noodles.

3 Cover the pan and simmer for 15 minutes. Add the spring onions and fresh coriander, season well with salt and freshly ground black pepper and cook gently for a further 5 minutes.

4 Meanwhile, heat the desiccated coconut and chilli in a small frying pan for 2–3 minutes, stirring frequently, until the coconut is lightly browned.

5 Pour the soup into bowls and serve sprinkled with the dry-fried coconut and chilli.

Chicken, Tomato and Christophene Soup

Chicken breasts and smoked haddock take on the flavours of herbs and spices to produce this well-flavoured soup.

INGREDIENTS

Serves 4

225 g/8 oz skinless, boneless chicken
   breasts, diced
1 garlic clove, crushed
a pinch of freshly grated nutmeg
25 g/1 oz/2 tbsp butter or margarine
½ onion, finely chopped
15 ml/1 tbsp tomato purée
400 g/14 oz can tomatoes, puréed
1.2 litres/2 pints/5 cups chicken stock
1 fresh chilli, seeded and chopped
1 christophene, peeled and diced (about
   350 g/12 oz)
5 ml/1 tsp dried oregano
2.5 ml/½ tsp dried thyme
50 g/2 oz smoked haddock fillet, skinned
   and diced
salt and freshly ground black pepper
snipped fresh chives, to garnish

1 Dice the chicken, place in a bowl and season with salt, pepper, garlic and nutmeg. Mix well to flavour and then set aside for about 30 minutes.

2 Melt the butter or margarine in a large saucepan, add the chicken and sauté over a moderate heat for 5–6 minutes. Stir in the onion and fry gently for a further 5 minutes or until the onion is slightly softened.

3 Add the tomato purée, puréed tomatoes, stock, chilli, christophene and herbs. Bring to the boil, cover and simmer gently for 35 minutes or until the christophene is tender.

4 Add the smoked fish and simmer for a further 5 minutes or until the fish is cooked through. Adjust the seasoning and pour into warmed soup bowls. Garnish with a scattering of snipped fresh chives and serve piping hot.

Chunky Chicken Soup

This thick chicken and vegetable soup is served with garlic-flavoured fried croûtons.

INGREDIENTS

Serves 4

4 skinless, boneless chicken thighs
15 g/½ oz/1 tbsp butter
2 small leeks, finely sliced
25 g/1 oz/2 tbsp long-grain rice
900 ml/ 1½ pints/3¾ cups chicken stock
15 ml/1 tbsp chopped mixed fresh parsley
   and mint
salt and freshly ground black pepper

For the garlic croûtons
30 ml/2 tbsp olive oil
1 garlic clove, crushed
4 slices bread, cut into cubes

1 Cut the chicken into 1 cm/ ½ in cubes. Melt the butter in a saucepan, add the leeks and cook until tender. Add the rice and chicken and cook for 2 minutes.

2 Add the stock, then cover the pan and simmer gently for 15–20 minutes until tender.

3 To make the garlic croûtons, heat the oil in a large frying pan. Add the crushed garlic clove and bread cubes and cook until the bread is golden brown, stirring all the time to prevent burning. Drain on kitchen paper and sprinkle with a pinch of salt.

4 Add the parsley and mint to the soup and adjust the seasoning to taste. Serve with the garlic croûtons.

Noodles in Soup

*In China, noodles in soup (*tang mein*) are far more popular than fried noodles (*chow mein*). You can adapt this basic recipe by using different ingredients for the "dressing".*

Serves 4

225 g/8 oz chicken breast fillet, pork fillet
    or ready-cooked meat
3–4 shiitake mushrooms, soaked
115 g/4 oz canned sliced bamboo
    shoots, drained
115 g/4 oz spinach leaves, lettuce hearts,
    or Chinese leaves
2 spring onions
350 g/12 oz dried egg noodles
600 ml/1 pint/2½ cups stock
30 ml/2 tbsp vegetable oil
5 ml/1 tsp salt
2.5 ml/½ tsp light brown sugar
15 ml/1 tbsp light soy sauce
10 ml/2 tsp Chinese rice wine or
    dry sherry
a few drops of sesame oil
red chilli sauce, to serve

1 Thinly shred the meat. Squeeze dry the shiitake mushrooms and discard any hard stalks. Then thinly shred the mushrooms, bamboo shoots, greens and spring onions.

2 Cook the noodles in boiling water according to the instructions on the packet, then drain and rinse under cold water. Place in a serving bowl.

3 Bring the stock to the boil and pour over the noodles. Set aside and keep warm.

4 Heat the oil in a preheated wok, add about half of the spring onions and the meat, and stir-fry for about 1 minute.

5 Add the mushrooms, bamboo shoots and greens and stir-fry for 1 minute. Add the salt, sugar, soy sauce and rice wine or sherry and blend well.

6 Pour the "dressing" over the noodles, garnish with the remaining spring onions, and sprinkle over a few drops of sesame oil. Divide into individual bowls and serve with red-chilli sauce.

Chiang Mai Noodle Soup

A signature dish of the city of Chiang Mai, this delicious noodle soup has Burmese origins and is the Thai equivalent of the Malaysian dish laksa.

INGREDIENTS

Serves 4–6

600 ml/1 pint/2½ cups coconut milk
30 ml/2 tbsp red curry paste
5 ml/1 tsp ground turmeric
450 g/1 lb chicken thighs, boned and cut
  into bite-size chunks
600 ml/1 pint/2½ cups chicken stock
60 ml/4 tbsp fish sauce
15 ml/1 tbsp dark soy sauce
juice of ½–1 lime
450 g/1 lb fresh egg noodles, blanched
  briefly in boiling water
salt and freshly ground black pepper

For the garnish
3 spring onions, chopped
4 fresh red chillies, chopped
4 shallots, chopped
60 ml/4 tbsp sliced pickled mustard
  leaves, rinsed
30 ml/2 tbsp fried sliced garlic
fresh coriander leaves
4 fried noodle nests (optional)

1 Pour about one-third of the coconut milk into a large saucepan and bring to the boil, stirring often with a wooden spoon until it separates.

2 Add the curry paste and ground turmeric, stir to mix together and cook until fragrant.

3 Add the chicken and stir-fry for about 2 minutes, ensuring that all the chunks are coated with the paste.

4 Add the remaining coconut milk, chicken stock, fish sauce and soy sauce. Season to taste and simmer gently for 7–10 minutes. Remove from the heat and stir in the lime juice.

5 Reheat the noodles in boiling water, drain and divide between individual bowls. Divide the chicken between the bowls and ladle in the hot soup. Top each serving of soup with a few of each of the garnishes.

Chicken Soup with Vermicelli

In Morocco, the cook – who is almost always the most senior female of the household – would use a whole chicken for this nourishing soup, to serve to her large extended family. This is a slightly simplified version, using chicken portions.

Serves 4–6

30 ml/2 tbsp sunflower oil

15 g/½ oz/1 tbsp butter

1 onion, chopped

2 chicken legs or breast pieces, halved
   or quartered

flour, for dusting

2 carrots, cut into 4 cm/1½ in pieces

1 parsnip, cut into 4 cm/1½ in pieces

1.5 litres/2½ pints/6¼ cups chicken stock

1 cinnamon stick

a good pinch of paprika

a pinch of saffron

2 egg yolks

juice of ½ lemon

30 ml/2 tbsp chopped fresh coriander

30 ml/2 tbsp chopped fresh parsley

150 g/5 oz vermicelli

salt and freshly ground black pepper

1 Heat the oil and butter in a saucepan or flameproof casserole, and fry the onion for 3–4 minutes until softened. Dust the chicken pieces in seasoned flour and fry gently until they are evenly browned.

2 Transfer the chicken to a plate and add the carrots and parsnip to the pan. Cook over a gentle heat for 3–4 minutes, stirring frequently, then return the chicken to the pan. Add the stock, cinnamon stick and paprika and season well with salt and pepper.

3 Bring the soup to the boil, cover and simmer for 1 hour until the vegetables are very tender.

4 Meanwhile, blend the saffron in 30 ml/2 tbsp boiling water. Beat the egg yolks with the lemon juice in a separate bowl and add the coriander and parsley. When the saffron water has cooled, stir into the egg and lemon mixture.

5 When the vegetables are tender, transfer the chicken to a plate. Spoon away any excess fat from the soup, then increase the heat a little and stir in the noodles. Cook for 5–6 minutes until the noodles are tender. Meanwhile, remove the skin and bones from the chicken and chop the flesh into bite-size pieces.

6 When the vermicelli is cooked stir in the chicken pieces and the egg, lemon and saffron mixture. Cook over a low heat for 1–2 minutes, stirring all the time. Adjust the seasoning and serve.

Mulligatawny Soup

Mulligatawny *(which literally means "pepper water") was introduced into England in the late 18th century by members of the colonial services returning home from India.*

INGREDIENTS

Serves 4

50 g/2 oz/4 tbsp butter or 60 ml/4 tbsp oil

2 large chicken joints (about 350 g/
   12 oz each)

1 onion, chopped

1 carrot, chopped

1 small turnip, chopped

about 15 ml/1 tbsp curry powder, to taste

4 cloves

6 black peppercorns, lightly crushed

50 g/2 oz/¼ cup lentils

900 ml/1½ pints/3¾ cups chicken stock

40 g/1½ oz/¼ cup sultanas

salt and freshly ground black pepper

1 Melt the butter or heat the oil in a large saucepan, then brown the chicken over a brisk heat. Transfer the chicken to a plate and set aside.

2 Add the onion, carrot and turnip to the pan and cook, stirring occasionally, until lightly coloured. Stir in the curry powder, cloves and crushed peppercorns and cook for 1–2 minutes, then add the lentils.

3 Pour the stock into the pan, bring to the boil, then add the sultanas, the chicken and any juices from the plate. Cover and simmer gently for about 1¼ hours.

COOK'S TIP

Choose red split lentils for the best colour, although either green or brown lentils could also be used.

4 Remove the chicken from the pan and discard the skin and bones. Chop the flesh, return to the soup and reheat. Check the seasoning before serving the soup piping hot.

Smoked Turkey and Lentil Soup

Lentils seem to enhance the flavour of smoked turkey, and combined with four tasty vegetables they make a fine meal-in-a-pot.

INGREDIENTS

Serves 4

25 g/1 oz/2 tbsp butter
1 large carrot, chopped
1 onion, chopped
1 leek, white part only, chopped
1 celery stick, chopped
115 g/4 oz/1½ cups mushrooms, chopped
50 ml/2 fl oz/¼ cup dry white wine
1.2 litres/2 pints/5 cups chicken stock
10 ml/2 tsp dried thyme
1 bay leaf
115 g/4 oz/½ cup lentils
75 g/3 oz smoked turkey meat, diced
salt and freshly ground black pepper

1 Melt the butter in a large saucepan. Add the carrot, onion, leek, celery and mushrooms. Cook for 3–5 minutes until golden.

2 Stir in the wine and chicken stock. Bring to the boil and skim off any foam that rises to the surface. Add the thyme and bay leaf. Lower the heat, cover and simmer gently for 30 minutes.

3 Add the lentils and continue cooking, covered, for a further 30–40 minutes until they are just tender. Stir the soup occasionally.

4 Add the turkey and season to taste with salt and pepper. Cook until just heated through. Ladle into bowls and serve.

Cock-a-leekie

This traditional soup recipe – it is known from as long ago as 1598 – originally included beef as well as chicken. In the olden days, it would have been made from an old cock bird, hence the name.

Serves 4

2 chicken portions, (about 275 g/10 oz each)
1.2 litres/2 pints/5 cups chicken stock
1 bouquet garni
4 leeks
8–12 prunes, soaked
salt and freshly ground black pepper
bread, to serve

1 Put the chicken portions into a saucepan with the stock and bouquet garni. Bring to the boil and simmer gently for 40 minutes.

2 Cut the white part of the leeks into 2.5 cm/1 in slices and finely slice a little of the green part.

3 Add the white part of the leeks and the prunes to the saucepan and cook gently for 20 minutes, then add the green part of the leeks and cook for a further 10–15 minutes.

4 Remove the bouquet garni and discard. Take the chicken out of the pan, discard the skin and bones, and chop the flesh. Return the chopped flesh to the pan and season the soup.

5 Heat the soup through gently. Ladle into warm soup bowls and serve hot with bread.

Scotch Broth

Sustaining and warming, Scotch Broth makes a delicious one-pot meal anywhere.

Serves 6

900 g/2 lb lean neck of lamb, cut into
    large, even-size chunks
1.75 litres/3 pints/7½ cups water
1 large onion, chopped
50 g/2 oz/¼ cup pearl barley
1 bouquet garni
1 large carrot, chopped
1 turnip, chopped
3 leeks, chopped
½ small white cabbage, shredded
salt and freshly ground black pepper
chopped fresh parsley, to
    garnish (optional)

1 Put the lamb and water into a large saucepan and bring to the boil. Skim off the scum, then stir in the onion, barley and bouquet garni.

2 Bring the soup back to the boil, then partly cover the saucepan and simmer gently for 1 hour. Add the remaining vegetables and the seasoning, bring back to the boil, partly cover again and simmer for about 35 minutes until the vegetables are tender.

3 Remove surplus fat from the top of the soup. Serve the soup hot, sprinkled with chopped parsley, if liked.

Lamb, Bean and Pumpkin Soup

This is a hearty soup to warm the cockles of the heart in even the chilliest weather.

INGREDIENTS

Serves 4

115 g/4 oz/²⁄₃ cup split black-eyed beans, soaked for 1–2 hours or overnight

675 g/1¹⁄₂ lb neck of lamb, cut into medium-size chunks

5 ml/1 tsp chopped fresh thyme or 2.5 ml/¹⁄₂ tsp dried thyme

2 bay leaves

1.2 litres/2 pints/5 cups stock or water

1 onion, sliced

225 g/8 oz pumpkin, diced

2 black cardamom pods

7.5 ml/1¹⁄₂ tsp ground turmeric

15 ml/1 tbsp chopped fresh coriander

2.5 ml/¹⁄₂ tsp caraway seeds

1 fresh green chilli, seeded and chopped

2 green bananas

1 carrot

salt and freshly ground black pepper

1 Drain the black-eyed beans, place them in a saucepan and cover with fresh cold water.

2 Bring the beans to the boil, boil rapidly for 10 minutes and then reduce the heat and simmer, covered, for about 40–50 minutes until tender, adding more water if necessary. Remove the pan from the heat and set aside to cool.

3 Meanwhile, put the lamb in a large saucepan, add the thyme, bay leaves and stock or water and bring to the boil. Cover and simmer over a moderate heat for 1 hour until tender.

4 Add the onion, pumpkin, cardamoms, turmeric, coriander, caraway, chilli and seasoning and stir. Bring back to a simmer and cook, uncovered, for 15 minutes, stirring occasionally, until the pumpkin is tender.

5 When the beans are cool, spoon into a blender or food processor with their liquid and blend to a smooth purée.

6 Peel the bananas and cut into medium slices. Cut the carrot into thin slices. Stir into the soup with the bean purée and cook for 10–12 minutes, until the carrot is tender. Adjust the seasoning and serve immediately.

Lamb and Lentil Soup

*Lamb and lentils go together so well,
they almost seem to have been made
for one another.*

Serves 4

About 1.5 litres/2½ pints/6¼ cups
water or stock
900 g/2 lb neck of lamb, cut into chops
½ onion, chopped
1 garlic clove, crushed
1 bay leaf
1 clove
2 sprigs of fresh thyme
225 g/8 oz potatoes, cut into
2.5 cm/1 in pieces
175 g/6 oz/¾ cup red lentils
salt and freshly ground black pepper
chopped fresh parsley

1 Put about 1.2 litres/2 pints/
5 cups of the stock or water
and the meat in a large saucepan
with the onion, garlic, bay leaf,
clove and sprigs of thyme. Bring
to the boil and simmer for about
1 hour until the lamb is tender.

COOK'S TIP

Red lentils do not need soaking
before they are cooked;
simply pick them over and
remove any pieces of grit
and debris, then rinse well.

2 Add the pieces of potato and
the lentils to the pan and
season the soup with a little salt
and plenty of black pepper. Add
the remaining stock or water to
come just above surface of the
meat and vegetables; you may
need more if the soup becomes
too thick during cooking.

3 Cover and allow to simmer for
25 minutes or until the lentils
are cooked and well blended into
the soup. Taste the soup and adjust
the seasoning as necessary. Stir in
the parsley and serve.

Moroccan Harira

This substantial meat and vegetable soup is traditionally eaten during the month of Ramadan, when the Muslim population fasts between sunrise and sunset.

INGREDIENTS

Serves 4

25 g/1 oz/2 tbsp butter
225 g/8 oz lamb, cut into 1 cm/½ in pieces
1 onion, chopped
450 g/1 lb well-flavoured tomatoes
60 ml/4 tbsp chopped fresh coriander
30 ml/2 tbsp chopped fresh parsley
2.5 ml/½ tsp ground turmeric
2.5 ml/½ tsp ground cinnamon
50 g/2 oz/¼ cup red lentils
75 g/3 oz/½ cup chick-peas,
   soaked overnight
600 ml/1 pint/2½ cups water
4 baby onions or small shallots, peeled
25 g/1 oz/¼ cup soup noodles
salt and freshly ground black pepper

For the garnish
chopped fresh coriander
lemon slices
ground cinnamon

1 Heat the butter in a large saucepan or flameproof casserole and fry the lamb and onion for 5 minutes, stirring frequently.

2 Peel the tomatoes, if you wish, by plunging them into boiling water to loosen the skins. Wait for them to cool a little before peeling off the skins. Then cut them into quarters and add to the lamb with the herbs and spices.

3 Rinse the lentils under cold running water and drain the chick-peas. Add both to the pan with the water. Season with salt and pepper. Bring to the boil, cover and simmer gently for 1½ hours.

4 Add the baby onions or small shallots and cook for a further 30 minutes. Add the noodles 5 minutes before the end of the cooking time. Serve the soup when the noodles are tender, garnished with the coriander, lemon slices and cinnamon.

Spinach and Lemon Soup with Meatballs

This soup, known as aarshe saak, *is almost standard fare in many parts of the Middle East. In Greece, it is made without the meatballs and is simply called* avgolemono.

INGREDIENTS

Serves 6

2 large onions
45 ml/3 tbsp oil
15 ml/1 tbsp ground turmeric
115 g/4 oz/½ cup yellow split peas
1.2 litres/2 pints/5 cups water
225 g/8 oz minced lamb
450 g/1 lb spinach, chopped
50 g/2 oz/½ cup rice flour
juice of 2 lemons
1–2 garlic cloves, finely chopped
30 ml/2 tbsp chopped fresh mint
4 eggs, beaten
salt and freshly ground black pepper
sprigs of fresh mint, to garnish

1 Chop one of the onions and fry in 30 ml/2 tbsp of the oil in a large pan until golden. Add the turmeric, peas and water and bring to the boil. Simmer for 20 minutes.

2 Grate the other onion into a bowl, add the lamb and seasoning and mix well. Using your hands, form the mixture into small balls, about the size of walnuts. Carefully add to the pan and simmer for 10 minutes, then add the spinach, cover and simmer for 20 minutes.

3 Mix the flour with about 250 ml/8 fl oz/1 cup cold water to make a smooth paste, then slowly add to the pan, stirring all the time. Add the lemon juice, season and cook over a gentle heat for 20 minutes.

4 Meanwhile, heat the remaining oil in a small pan and fry the garlic briefly until golden. Stir in the mint and remove the pan from the heat.

5 Remove the soup from the heat and stir in the beaten eggs. Sprinkle the prepared garlic and mint mixture over the soup, garnish with mint sprigs and serve immediately.

Bean and Pasta Soup

This hearty, main-meal soup sometimes goes by the simpler name of pasta e fagioli, *while some Italians refer to it as* minestrone di pasta e fagioli. *Traditional recipes use dried beans and a ham bone.*

INGREDIENTS

Serves 4–6

30 ml/2 tbsp olive oil

115 g/4 oz/²⁄₃ cup pancetta or rindless smoked streaky bacon, diced

1 onion

1 carrot

1 celery stick

1.75 litres/3 pints/7½ cups beef stock

1 cinnamon stick or a good pinch of ground cinnamon

90 g/3½ oz/scant 1 cup small pasta shapes, such as conchiglie or coralini

400 g/14 oz can borlotti beans, rinsed and drained

1 thick slice cooked ham (about 225 g/ 8 oz) diced

salt and freshly ground black pepper

Parmesan cheese shavings, to serve

1 Heat the oil in a large saucepan, add the pancetta or bacon and cook, stirring, until lightly coloured. Finely chop the vegetables, add to the pan and cook for about 10 minutes, stirring frequently, until lightly coloured. Pour in the stock, add the cinnamon with salt and pepper to taste and bring to the boil. Cover and simmer gently for 15–20 minutes.

2 Add the pasta shapes. Bring back to the boil, stirring all the time. Lower the heat and simmer, stirring frequently, for 5 minutes. Add the borlotti beans and diced ham and simmer for 2–3 minutes, or according to the instructions on the packet, until the pasta is *al dente*.

3 Remove the cinnamon stick, if used, taste the soup and adjust the seasoning. Serve hot in warmed bowls, sprinkled with Parmesan shavings.

VARIATION

If you prefer, you can use spaghetti or tagliatelle instead of the small pasta shapes, breaking it into small pieces over the pan. Use cannellini or white haricot beans instead of the borlotti. Add them to the pan after the stock in step 1. If you like, add 15 ml/1 tbsp tomato purée along with the beans.

Bacon and Lentil Soup

Serve this hearty soup with chunks of warm, crusty bread.

INGREDIENTS

Serves 4

450 g/1 lb thick-sliced bacon, cubed

1 onion, roughly chopped

1 small turnip, roughly chopped

1 celery stick, chopped

1 potato, roughly chopped

1 carrot, sliced

75 g/3 oz/scant ¹⁄₂ cup lentils

1 bouquet garni

freshly ground black pepper

fresh flat-leaf parsley, to garnish

1 Heat a large pan and add the bacon. Cook for a few minutes, allowing the fat to run out.

2 Add the chopped onion, turnip, celery and potato and the sliced carrot. Cook for 4 minutes, stirring from time to time.

3 Add the lentils, bouquet garni, seasoning and enough water to cover. Bring to the boil and simmer for 1 hour or until the lentils are tender. Pour the soup into warmed bowls and serve garnished with flat-leaf parsley.

Noodle Soup with Pork and Szechuan Pickle

This soup is a meal in itself and the hot pickle gives it a delicious tang.

INGREDIENTS

Serves 4

1 litre/1¾ pints/4 cups chicken stock
350 g/12 oz egg noodles
15 ml/1 tbsp dried prawns, soaked in water
30 ml/2 tbsp vegetable oil
225 g/8 oz lean pork, finely shredded
15 ml/1 tbsp yellow bean paste
15 ml/1 tbsp soy sauce
115 g/4 oz Szechuan hot pickle, rinsed, drained and shredded
a pinch of sugar
2 spring onions, finely sliced, to garnish

1 Bring the stock to the boil in a saucepan. Add the noodles and cook until almost tender. Drain the noodles. Drain the dried prawns, rinse them under cold water, drain again and add to the stock. Lower the heat and simmer for a further 2 minutes. Keep hot.

2 Heat the oil in a frying pan or wok. Add the pork and stir-fry over a high heat for 3 minutes.

3 Add the bean paste and soy sauce to the pork and stir-fry for 1 minute. Add the hot pickle with a pinch of sugar. Stir-fry for 1 minute further.

4 Divide the noodles and soup among individual serving bowls. Spoon the pork mixture on top, then sprinkle with the spring onions and serve at once.

Galician Broth

This delicious main-meal soup is very similar to the warming, chunky meat and potato broths of cooler climates. For extra colour, a few onion skins can be added when cooking the gammon, but remember to remove them before serving.

INGREDIENTS

Serves 4

450 g/1 lb piece gammon
2 bay leaves
2 onions, sliced
1.5 litres/2½ pints/6¼ cups cold water
10 ml/2 tsp paprika
675 g/1½ lb potatoes, cut into large chunks
225 g/8 oz spring greens
400 g/14 oz can haricot or cannellini
   beans, drained
salt and freshly ground black pepper

1 Soak the gammon overnight in cold water. Drain and put in a large saucepan with the bay leaves and onions. Pour the water on top.

2 Bring to the boil, then reduce the heat and simmer gently for about 1½ hours until the meat is tender. Keep an eye on the pan to make sure it doesn't boil over.

COOK'S TIP
~
Bacon knuckles can be used instead of the gammon. The bones will give the juices a delicious flavour.

3 Drain the meat, reserving the cooking liquid, and leave to cool slightly. Discard the skin and any excess fat from the meat and cut into small chunks. Return to the pan with the cooking liquid, paprika and potatoes. Cover and simmer gently for 20 minutes.

4 Cut away the cores from the greens. Roll up the leaves and cut into thin shreds. Add to the pan with the beans and simmer for about 10 minutes. Season with salt and freshly ground black pepper to taste and serve piping hot.

Seafood and Sausage Gumbo

Gumbo is a soup but is often served over rice as a main course.

Serves 10–12

1.5 kg/3 lbs raw prawns in shell
1.5 litres/2½ pints/6¼ cups water
4 medium onions, 2 of them quartered
4 bay leaves
175 ml/6 fl oz/¾ cup vegetable oil
115 g/4 oz/1 cup flour
60 ml/4 tbsp margarine or butter
2 green peppers, seeded and
 finely chopped
4 celery sticks, finely chopped
675 g/1½ lb Polish or andouille sausage,
 cut into 1 cm/½ in slices
450 g/1 lb fresh okra, cut into 1 cm/
 ½ in slices
3 garlic cloves, crushed
2.5 ml/½ tsp fresh or dried thyme leaves
10 ml/2 tsp salt
2.5 ml/½ tsp freshly ground black pepper
2.5 ml/½ tsp white pepper
5 ml/1 tsp cayenne pepper
475 ml/16 fl oz hot pepper
 sauce (optional)
2 cups chopped, peeled, fresh or canned
 plum tomatoes
450 g/1 lb fresh crab meat
boiled rice, to serve

1 Peel and devein the prawns; reserve the heads and shells. Cover and chill the prawns while you make the sauce.

2 Place the prawn heads and shells in a saucepan with the water, quartered onion and 1 bay leaf. Bring to the boil, then partly cover and simmer for 20 minutes. Strain and set aside.

3 To make a Cajun roux, heat the oil in a heavy-based frying pan. When the oil is hot, add the flour, a little at a time, and blend to a smooth paste.

4 Cook over a medium-low heat, stirring constantly for 25–40 minutes until the roux reaches the colour of peanut butter. Remove the pan from the heat and continue stirring until the roux has cooled and stopped cooking.

5 Melt the margarine or butter in a large, heavy-based saucepan or flameproof casserole. Finely chop the remaining onions and add to the pan with the peppers and celery. Cook over a medium-low heat for 6–8 minutes until the onions are softened, stirring occasionally.

6 Add the sausage and mix well. Cook for 5 minutes more. Add the okra and garlic, stir, and cook until the okra stops producing white "threads".

7 Add the remaining bay leaves, the thyme, salt, black and white peppers, cayenne pepper, and hot pepper sauce to taste, if using. Mix well. Stir in 1.35 litres/ 2¼ pints/6 cups of the prawn stock and the tomatoes. Bring to the boil, partly cover the pan, lower the heat and simmer for about 20 minutes.

8 Whisk in the Cajun roux. Raise the heat and bring to the boil, whisking well. Lower the heat again and simmer, uncovered, for a further 40–45 minutes, stirring occasionally.

9 Gently stir in the prawns and crab meat. Cook for 3–4 minutes until the prawns turn pink.

10 To serve, put a mound of hot boiled rice in each serving bowl and ladle on the gumbo, making sure each person gets some prawns, some crab meat and some sausage.

Green Herb Gumbo

Traditionally served at the end of Lent, this is a joyful, sweetly spiced and revitalizing dish, even if you haven't been fasting. The variety of green ingredients is important, so buy substitutes if you cannot find all of them.

INGREDIENTS

Serves 6–8

350 g/12 oz piece raw smoked gammon
30 ml/2 tbsp lard or cooking oil
1 large Spanish onion, roughly chopped
2–3 garlic cloves, crushed
5 ml/1 tsp dried oregano
5 ml/1 tsp dried thyme
2 bay leaves
2 cloves
2 celery sticks, finely sliced
1 green pepper, seeded and chopped
1/2 medium green cabbage, stalked and
    finely shredded
2 litres/3 1/2 pints/9 cups light stock or
    water
200 g/7 oz spring greens or kale, finely
    shredded
200 g/7 oz Chinese mustard cabbage,
    finely shredded
200 g/7 oz spinach, shredded
1 bunch of watercress, shredded
6 spring onions, finely shredded
25 g/1 oz/1/2 cup chopped fresh parsley
2.5 ml/1/2 tsp ground allspice
1/4 nutmeg, grated
a pinch of cayenne pepper
salt and freshly ground black pepper

1 Dice the ham quite small, keeping any fat and rind in one separate piece. Put the fat piece with the lard or oil into a deep saucepan and heat until it sizzles. Stir in the diced ham, onion, garlic, oregano and thyme and cook over a medium heat for 5 minutes, stirring occasionally.

2 Add the bay leaves, cloves, celery and green pepper and stir over a medium heat for another 2–3 minutes, then add the cabbage and stock or water. Bring to the boil and simmer gently for 5 minutes.

3 Add the spring greens or kale and mustard cabbage, boil for a further 2 minutes, then add the spinach, watercress and spring onions. Return to the boil, then lower the heat and simmer for 1 minute. Add the parsley, allspice and nutmeg, salt, black pepper and cayenne to taste.

4 Remove the piece of ham fat and, if you can find them, the cloves. Ladle into individual soup bowls and serve immediately, with warm French bread or garlic bread.

Beef and Herb Soup with Yogurt

This classic Iranian soup, aashe
maste, *is a meal in itself and is a
popular cold-weather dish.*

INGREDIENTS

Serves 4

2 large onions

30 ml/2 tbsp oil

15 ml/1 tbsp ground turmeric

90 g/3½ oz/scant ½ cup yellow split peas

1.2 litres/2 pints/5 cups water

225 g/8 oz minced beef

200 g/7 oz/1 cup rice

45 ml/3 tbsp each chopped fresh parsley,
    coriander and chives

15 g/½ oz/1 tbsp butter

1 large garlic clove, finely chopped

60 ml/4 tbsp chopped fresh mint

2–3 saffron strands dissolved in
    15 ml/1 tbsp boiling water (optional)

salt and freshly ground black pepper

natural yogurt and naan bread, to serve

fresh mint, to garnish

1 Chop one of the onions. Heat
the oil in a large saucepan and
fry the chopped onion until golden
brown. Add the turmeric, split
peas and water, bring to the boil,
then reduce the heat and simmer
for 20 minutes.

2 Grate the other onion into a
bowl, add the minced beef and
seasoning and mix well. Using
your hands, form the mixture into
small balls about the size of
walnuts. Carefully add to the pan
and simmer for 10 minutes.

3 Add the rice, parsley, coriander
and chives. Simmer for about
30 minutes until the rice is tender,
stirring frequently.

4 Melt the butter in a small pan
and gently fry the garlic. Stir
in the mint and sprinkle the soup
with the saffron, if using.

5 Spoon the soup into warmed
serving dishes. Garnish with
mint and serve with yogurt and
naan bread.

COOK'S TIP

Fresh spinach is also delicious in
this soup. Add 50 g/2 oz finely
chopped spinach leaves along
with the parsley, coriander
and chives.

Beef Noodle Soup

Offer your fortunate friends or family a steaming bowl of this soup, packed with delicious flavours of the Orient.

INGREDIENTS

Serves 4

10 g/¼ oz dried porcini mushrooms

150 ml/¼ pint/⅔ cup boiling water

6 spring onions

115 g/4 oz carrots

350 g/12 oz rump steak

about 30 ml/2 tbsp oil

1 garlic clove, crushed

2.5 cm/1 in piece fresh root ginger, peeled
  and finely chopped

1.2 litres/2 pints/5 cups beef stock

45 ml/3 tbsp light soy sauce

60 ml/4 tbsp dry sherry

75 g/3 oz thin egg noodles

75 g/3 oz spinach, shredded

salt and freshly ground black pepper

1 Break the mushrooms into small pieces, place in a bowl and pour over the boiling water. Leave to soak for 15 minutes.

2 Shred the spring onions and carrots into 5 cm/2 in long, fine strips. Trim any fat off the meat and slice into thin strips.

3 Heat the oil in a large saucepan and cook the beef in batches until browned, adding a little more oil if necessary. Remove the beef with a slotted spoon and drain on kitchen paper.

4 Add the garlic, ginger, spring onions and carrots to the pan and stir-fry for 3 minutes.

5 Add the beef, beef stock, the mushrooms and their soaking liquid, soy sauce and sherry. Season generously with salt and freshly ground black pepper. Bring to the boil and simmer, covered, for 10 minutes.

6 Break up the noodles slightly and add to the pan with the shredded spinach. Simmer gently for 5 minutes until the beef is tender. Adjust the seasoning to taste before serving.

COOK'S TIP

Dried porcini mushrooms are now widely available in supermarkets. They may seem expensive, but are full of flavour, so a small quantity goes a long way and really gives a lift to a soup like this one.

Vegetable Broth with Minced Beef

This is a veritable cornucopia of flavours, combining to produce a rich and satisfying broth.

Serves 6

30 ml/2 tbsp groundnut oil

115 g/4 oz finely minced beef

1 large onion, grated or finely chopped

1 garlic clove, crushed

1–2 fresh chillies, seeded and chopped

1 cm/½ in cube terasi, prepared

3 macadamia nuts or 6 almonds, finely ground

1 carrot, finely grated

5 ml/1 tsp brown sugar

1 litre/1¾ pints/4 cups chicken stock

50 g/2 oz dried shrimps, soaked in warm water for 10 minutes

225 g/8 oz spinach, finely shredded

8 baby sweetcorn, sliced, or 200 g/7 oz canned sweetcorn kernels

1 large tomato, chopped

juice of ½ lemon

salt

1 Heat the oil in a saucepan. Add the beef, onion and garlic and cook, stirring, until the meat changes colour.

2 Add the chillies, terasi, macadamia nuts or almonds, carrot, sugar and salt to taste.

3 Add the stock and bring gently to the boil. Reduce the heat to a simmer and then add the soaked shrimps, with their soaking liquid. Simmer for about 10 minutes.

4 A few minutes before serving, add the spinach, sweetcorn, tomato and lemon juice. Simmer for 1–2 minutes, to heat through. Do not overcook at this stage because this will spoil both the appearance and the taste of the end result. Serve at once.

COOK'S TIP

To make this broth very hot and spicy, add the seeds from the chillies.

Beef Broth with Cassava

*This "big" soup is almost like a
stew. The addition of wine is not
traditional, but enhances the
richness of the broth.*

INGREDIENTS

Serves 4

450 g/1 lb stewing beef, cubed

1.2 litres/2 pints/5 cups beef stock

300 ml/½ pint/1¼ cups white wine

15 ml/1 tbsp soft brown sugar

1 onion, finely chopped

1 bay leaf

1 bouquet garni

1 sprig of fresh thyme

15 ml/1 tbsp tomato purée

1 large carrot, sliced

275 g/10 oz cassava or yam, cubed

50 g/2 oz spinach, chopped

a little hot pepper sauce, to taste

salt and freshly ground black pepper

2 Add the carrot, cassava or
yam, spinach, a few drops of
hot pepper sauce, salt and pepper,
and simmer for a further
15 minutes until both the meat
and vegetables are tender. Serve.

COOK'S TIP

If you like, a cheap cut of lamb
can be used instead of beef,
and any other root vegetable can
be used instead of, or as well as,
the cassava or yam. Noodles,
pasta shapes or macaroni can
also be used as a base, in which
case you can cut down on the
root vegetables. You can, if you
prefer, omit the wine and
add more water.

1 Put the beef, stock, wine,
sugar, onion, bay leaf, bouquet
garni, thyme and tomato purée in
a large saucepan, bring to the boil
and then cover and simmer for
about 1¼ hours.

SPECIAL
OCCASION
SOUPS

~

Melon and Basil Soup

This is a deliciously refreshing, chilled fruit soup, just right for a hot summer's day.

INGREDIENTS

Serves 4–6

2 Charentais or rock melons

75 g/3 oz/scant ½ cup caster sugar

175 ml/6 fl oz/¾ cup water

finely grated rind and juice of 1 lime

45 ml/3 tbsp shredded fresh basil, plus
   whole leaves, to garnish

2 Place the sugar, water and lim rind in a small pan over a low heat. Stir until dissolved, bring to the boil and simmer for 2–3 minutes. Remove from the heat and leave to cool slightly. Pou half the mixture into the blender or food processor with the melon flesh. Blend until smooth, adding the remaining syrup and lime juice to taste.

3 Pour the mixture into a bowl, stir in the shredded basil and chill. Serve garnished with whole basil leaves and the reserved melon balls.

1 Cut the melons in half across the middle. Scrape out the seeds and discard. Using a melon baller, scoop out 20–24 balls and set aside for the garnish. Scoop out the remaining flesh and place in a blender or food processor.

COOK'S TIP

Add the syrup in two stages, as the amount of sugar needed will depend on the sweetness of the melon.

Red Onion and Beetroot Soup

V

This beautiful, ruby-red soup, with its contrasting swirl of yogurt, will look stunning at any dinner party.

Serves 4–6

15 ml/1 tbsp olive oil

350 g/12 oz red onions, sliced

2 garlic cloves, crushed

275 g/10 oz cooked beetroot, cut into sticks

1.2 litres/2 pints/5 cups vegetable stock
 or water

50 g/2 oz/1 cup cooked soup pasta

30 ml/2 tbsp raspberry vinegar

salt and freshly ground black pepper

natural yogurt or fromage blanc and
 snipped fresh chives, to garnish

2 Cook gently for about 20 minutes or until soft and tender, stirring occasionally.

3 Add the beetroot, stock or water, cooked pasta and vinegar and heat through. Season and garnish with swirls of yogurt or fromage blanc and chives.

1 Heat the olive oil in a large saucepan or flameproof casserole and add the onions and garlic.

COOK'S TIP

Try substituting cooked barley
for the pasta to give extra
nuttiness to the flavour.

Beetroot Soup with Ravioli

*Beetroot and pasta make an
unusual combination, but this
soup is no less good for that.*

Serves 4–6

1 quantity of basic pasta dough
1 egg white, beaten, for brushing
flour, for dusting
1 small onion or shallot, finely chopped
2 garlic cloves, crushed
5 ml/1 tsp fennel seeds
600 ml/1 pint/2¹/₂ cups chicken or
   vegetable stock
225 g/8 oz cooked beetroot
30 ml/2 tbsp fresh orange juice
fresh fennel or dill leaves, to garnish
crusty bread, to serve

For the filling

115 g/4 oz mushrooms, finely chopped
1 shallot or small onion, finely chopped
1–2 garlic cloves, crushed
5 ml/1 tsp chopped fresh thyme
15 ml/1 tbsp chopped fresh parsley
90 ml/6 tbsp fresh white breadcrumbs
salt and freshly ground black pepper
a large pinch of freshly grated nutmeg

1 Put all the filling ingredients
in a food processor or blender
and process to a paste.

2 Roll the pasta into thin sheets.
Lay one piece over a ravioli
tray and put 5 ml/1 tsp of the
filling into each depression. Brush
around the edges of each ravioli
with egg white. Cover with another
sheet of pasta and press the edges
together well to seal. Transfer to
a floured tea towel and rest for
one hour before cooking.

3 Cook the ravioli boiling, salted
water for 2 minutes. (Cook in
batches to stop them sticking
together.) Remove and drop into a
bowl of cold water for 5 seconds
before placing on a tray. (You can
make these pasta shapes a day in
advance and store in the fridge.)

4 Put the onion, garlic and
fennel seeds into a pan with
150 ml/¹/₄ pint/²/₃ cup of the stock.
Bring to the boil, cover and
simmer for 5 minutes until tender.
Peel and finely dice the beetroot,
reserving 60 ml/4 tbsp for the
garnish. Add the rest of it to the
soup with the remaining stock,
and bring to the boil.

5 Add the orange juice and
cooked ravioli and simmer
for 2 minutes. Serve in shallow
soup bowls, garnished with the
reserved diced beetroot and fresh
fennel or dill leaves. Serve hot,
with crusty bread.

Italian Vegetable Soup

V

The success of this clear soup depends on the quality of the stock, so use home-made vegetable stock rather than stock cubes.

INGREDIENTS

Serves 4

1 small carrot

l baby leek

1 celery stick

50 g/2 oz green cabbage

900 ml/1½ pints/3¾ cups vegetable stock

1 bay leaf

115 g/4 oz/1 cup cooked cannellini beans

25 g/1 oz/¼ cup soup pasta, such as tiny shells, bows, stars or elbows

salt and freshly ground black pepper

snipped fresh chives, to garnish

1 Cut the carrot, leek and celery into 5 cm/2 in long julienne strips. Finely shred the cabbage.

2 Put the stock and bay leaf into a large saucepan and bring to the boil. Add the carrot, leek and celery, cover and simmer for 6 minutes, until the vegetables are softened, but not tender.

3 Add the cabbage, beans and pasta, then simmer, uncovered, for a further 4–5 minutes, or until the vegetables are tender and the pasta is *al dente*.

4 Remove the bay leaf and season to taste. Ladle the soup into four warmed soup bowls and garnish with snipped chives. Serve immediately.

Butternut Squash Bisque

This is a fragrant, creamy and delicately flavoured soup.

INGREDIENTS

Serves 4

25 g/1 oz/2 tbsp butter or margarine

2 small onions, finely chopped

450 g/1 lb butternut squash, peeled, seeded and cubed

1.2 litres/2 pints/5 cups chicken stock

225 g/8 oz potatoes, cubed

5 ml/1 tsp paprika

120 ml/4 fl oz/½ cup whipping cream (optional)

25 ml/1½ tbsp chopped fresh chives, plus a few whole chives to garnish

salt and freshly ground black pepper

1 Melt the butter or margarine in a large saucepan. Add the onions and cook for about 5 minutes until soft.

2 Add the squash, stock, potatoes and paprika. Bring to the boil. Reduce the heat to low, cover the pan and simmer for about 35 minutes until all the vegetables are soft.

3 Pour the soup into a food processor or blender and process until smooth. Return the soup to the pan and stir in the cream, if using. Season with salt and pepper. Reheat gently.

4 Stir in the chopped chives just before serving. Garnish each serving with a few whole chives.

Red Pepper Soup with Lime

The beautiful, rich red colour of this soup makes it an attractive starter or light lunch. For a special dinner, toast some tiny croûtons and serve these sprinkled into the soup.

INGREDIENTS

Serves 4–6

1 large onion, chopped
4 red peppers, seeded and chopped
5 ml/1 tsp olive oil
1 garlic clove, crushed
1 small fresh red chilli, sliced
45 ml/3 tbsp tomato purée
900 ml/1½ pints/3¾ cups chicken stock
finely grated rind and juice of 1 lime
salt and freshly ground black pepper
shreds of lime rind, to garnish

1 Cook the onion and peppers gently in the oil in a covered saucepan for about 5 minutes, shaking the pan occasionally, until just softened.

2 Stir in the garlic, chilli and tomato purée. Add half the stock, then bring to the boil. Cover and simmer for 10 minutes.

3 Cool slightly, then purée in a food processor or blender. Return to the pan and add the remaining stock, the lime rind and juice and salt and pepper.

4 Bring the soup back to the boil, then serve at once, with a few strips of lime rind scattered into each bowl.

Tomato and Fresh Basil Soup

This is the perfect soup for late summer when fresh tomatoes are at their most flavoursome.

INGREDIENTS

Serves 4–6

15 ml/1 tbsp olive oil

25 g/1 oz/2 tbsp butter

1 medium onion, finely chopped

900 g/2 lb ripe Italian plum tomatoes, roughly chopped

1 garlic clove, roughly chopped

about 750 ml/1¼ pints/3 cups chicken or vegetable stock

120 ml/4 fl oz/½ cup dry white wine

30 ml/2 tbsp sun-dried tomato purée

30 ml/2 tbsp shredded fresh basil, plus a few whole leaves to garnish

150 ml/¼ pint/ ⅔ cup double cream

salt and freshly ground black pepper

1 Heat the oil and butter in a large saucepan until foaming. Add the onion and cook gently for about 5 minutes, stirring frequently, until softened, but do not allow to brown.

2 Stir in the chopped tomatoes and garlic, then add the stock, white wine and sun-dried tomato purée, with salt and pepper to taste. Bring to the boil, then lower the heat, half-cover the pan and simmer gently for 20 minutes, stirring occasionally to stop the tomatoes sticking to the base.

3 Process the soup with the shredded basil in a food processor or blender, then press through a sieve into a clean pan.

4 Add the double cream and heat through, stirring. Do not allow the soup to approach boiling point. Check the consistency and add more stock, if necessary. Adjust the seasoning to taste, pour into heated bowls and garnish with whole basil leaves. Serve at once.

Wild Mushroom Soup

Wild mushrooms are expensive.
Dried porcini have an intense
flavour, so only a small quantity is
needed. The beef stock may seem
unusual in a vegetable soup, but it
helps to strengthen the earthy
flavour of the mushrooms.

INGREDIENTS

Serves 4

25 g/1 oz/2 cups dried porcini mushrooms
250 ml/8 fl oz/1 cup warm water
30 ml/2 tbsp olive oil
15 g/¹/₂ oz/1 tbsp butter
2 leeks, finely sliced
2 shallots, roughly chopped
1 garlic clove, roughly chopped
225 g/8 oz fresh wild mushrooms
1.2 litres/2 pints/5 cups beef stock
2.5 ml/¹/₂ tsp dried thyme
150 ml/¹/₄ pint/²/₃ cup double cream
salt and freshly ground black pepper
sprigs of fresh thyme, to garnish

3 Chop or slice the fresh
mushrooms and add to the
pan. Stir over a medium heat for
a few minutes until they begin
to soften. Pour in the beef stock
and bring to the boil. Add the
porcini, soaking liquid, dried
thyme and salt and pepper. Lower
the heat, half-cover the pan and
simmer gently for 30 minutes,
stirring occasionally.

4 Pour about three-quarters
of the soup into a food
processor or blender and process
until smooth. Return to the soup
remaining in the pan, stir in the
double cream and heat through.
Check the consistency, adding
more stock or water if the soup
is too thick. Adjust the seasoning.
Serve hot, garnished with sprigs
of fresh thyme.

1 Put the dried porcini in a
bowl, add the warm water and
leave to soak for 20–30 minutes.
Lift out of the liquid and squeeze
to remove as much of the soaking
liquid as possible. Strain all the
liquid and reserve to use later.
Finely chop the porcini.

2 Heat the oil and butter in a
large saucepan until foaming.
Add the leeks, shallots and garlic
and cook gently for about
5 minutes, stirring frequently,
until softened but not coloured.

V

Hungarian Sour Cherry Soup

Particularly popular in summer, this fruit soup is typical of Hungarian cooking. The recipe makes good use of plump, sour cherries. Fruit soups are thickened with flour, and a touch of salt is added to help bring out the flavour of the cold soup.

INGREDIENTS

Serves 4

15 ml/1 tbsp plain flour

120 ml/4 fl oz/½ cup soured cream

a generous pinch of salt

5 ml/1 tsp caster sugar

225 g/8 oz/1½ cups fresh sour or morello cherries, stoned

900 ml/1½ pints/3¾ cups water

50 g/2 oz/¼ cup granulated sugar

1 In a bowl, blend the flour with the soured cream until smooth, then add the salt and caster sugar.

2 Put the cherries in a pan with the water and granulated sugar. Gently poach for about 10 minutes.

3 Remove from the heat and set aside 30 ml/2 tbsp of the cooking liquid as a garnish. Stir another 30 ml/2 tbsp of the cherry liquid into the flour and soured cream mixture, then pour this on to the cherries.

4 Return to the heat. Bring to the boil, then simmer gently for 5–6 minutes.

5 Remove from the heat, cover with clear film and leave to cool. Add extra salt if necessary. Serve with the reserved cooking liquid swirled in.

Apple Soup

A delicious soup that makes the most of freshly-picked apples.

INGREDIENTS

Serves 6

45 ml/3 tbsp oil

1 kohlrabi, diced

3 carrots, diced

2 celery sticks, diced

1 green pepper, seeded and diced

2 tomatoes, diced

2 litres/3½ pints/9 cups chicken stock

6 large green apples

45 ml/3 tbsp plain flour

150 ml/¼ pint/⅔ cup double cream

15 ml/1 tbsp granulated sugar

30–45 ml/2–3 tbsp lemon juice

salt and freshly ground black pepper

lemon wedges and crusty bread, to serve

1 Heat the oil in a large saucepan. Add the kohlrabi, carrots, celery, green pepper and tomatoes and fry for 5–6 minutes until just softened.

2 Pour in the chicken stock, bring to the boil, then reduce the heat and simmer for about 45 minutes.

3 Meanwhile, peel and core the apples, then chop into small cubes. Add to the pan and simmer for a further 15 minutes.

4 In a bowl, mix together the flour and cream, then pour slowly into the soup, stirring well, and bring to the boil. Add the sugar and lemon juice before seasoning. Serve immediately with lemon wedges and crusty bread.

V

Hot-and-sour Soup

A classic Chinese soup, this is a warming and flavoursome start to a meal.

Serves 4

10 g/¼ oz dried cloud ears

8 fresh shiitake mushrooms

75 g/3 oz tofu

50 g/2 oz/½ cup sliced, drained, canned
   bamboo shoots

900 ml/1½ pints/3¾ cups vegetable stock

15 ml/1 tbsp caster sugar

45 ml/3 tbsp rice vinegar

15 ml/1 tbsp light soy sauce

1.5 ml/¼ tsp chilli oil

2.5 ml/½ tsp salt

a large pinch of freshly ground white
   pepper

15 ml/1 tbsp cornflour

15 ml/l tbsp cold water

1 egg white

5 ml/1 tsp sesame oil

2 spring onions, cut into fine rings,
   to garnish

COOK'S TIP

~

To transform this tasty soup into
a nutritious light meal, simply
add extra mushrooms, tofu
and bamboo shoots.

1 Soak the cloud ears in hot
water for 30 minutes or until
soft. Drain, trim off and discard
the hard base from each, and chop
the cloud ears roughly.

2 Remove and discard the stalks
from the shiitake mushrooms.
Cut the caps into thin strips. Cut
the tofu into 1 cm/½ in cubes and
shred the bamboo shoots finely.

3 Place the stock, mushrooms,
tofu, bamboo shoots and
cloud ears in a large saucepan.
Bring the stock to the boil, lower
the heat and simmer for about
5 minutes.

4 Stir in the sugar, vinegar, soy
sauce, chilli oil, salt and
pepper. Mix the cornflour to a
paste with the water. Add the
mixture to the soup, stirring until
it thickens slightly.

5 Lightly beat the egg white,
then pour it slowly into the
soup in a steady stream, stirring
constantly. Cook, stirring, until the
egg white changes colour.

6 Add the sesame oil just before
serving. Ladle into heated
bowls and garnish each portion
with spring onion rings.

Pear and Watercress Soup

This unusual soup combines sweet pears with slightly sharp watercress. A more traditional partner, Stilton cheese, appears in the form of crisp croûtons.

INGREDIENTS

Serves 6

1 bunch of watercress

4 medium pears, sliced

900 ml/1½ pints/3¾ cups chicken stock, preferably home-made

120 ml/4 fl oz/½ cup double cream

juice of 1 lime

salt and freshly ground black pepper

For the Stilton croûtons

25 g/1 oz/2 tbsp butter

15 ml/1 tbsp olive oil

200 g/7 oz/3 cups cubed stale bread

115 g/4 oz/1 cup Stilton cheese, chopped

1 Place two-thirds of the watercress leaves and all the stalks in a pan with the pears, stock and a little seasoning. Simmer for about 15–20 minutes.

2 Reserving some of the watercress leaves for the garnish, add the rest to the soup and immediately blend in a food processor until smooth.

3 Put the mixture into a bowl and stir in the cream and the lime juice to mix the flavours thoroughly. Season again to taste. Pour all the soup back into the pan and reheat, stirring gently, until warmed through.

4 To make the Stilton croûtons, melt the butter and oil and fry the cubes of bread until golden brown. Drain on kitchen paper. Put the cheese on top and heat under a hot grill until bubbling.

5 Pour the soup into warmed bowls. Divide the croûtons and reserved watercress among the bowls and serve.

Star-gazer Vegetable Soup

V

If you have the time, it is worth making your own stock – either vegetable or, if preferred, chicken or fish – for this recipe.

INGREDIENTS

Serves 4

1 yellow pepper
2 large courgettes
2 large carrots
1 kohlrabi
900 ml/1½ pints/3¾ cups well-flavoured
   vegetable stock
50 g/2 oz rice vermicelli
salt and freshly ground black pepper

1 Cut the pepper into quarters, removing the seeds and core. Cut the courgettes and carrots lengthways into 5 mm/¼ in slices and slice the kohlrabi into 5 mm/¼ in rounds.

2 Using tiny pastry cutters, stamp out shapes from the vegetables or use a very sharp knife to cut the sliced vegetables into stars and other decorative shapes.

COOK'S TIP

Sauté the leftover vegetable pieces in a little oil and mix with cooked brown rice to make a tasty risotto.

3 Place the vegetables and stock in a pan and simmer for 10 minutes, until the vegetables are tender. Season to taste with salt and pepper.

4 Meanwhile, place the vermicelli in a bowl, cover with boiling water and set aside for 4 minutes. Drain, then divide among four warmed soup bowls. Ladle over the soup and serve.

V

Spinach and Rice Soup

Use very fresh, young spinach leaves and risotto rice to prepare this surprisingly light, refreshing soup.

INGREDIENTS

Serves 4

675 g/1½ lb fresh spinach, washed
45 ml/3 tbsp extra-virgin olive oil
1 small onion, finely chopped
2 garlic cloves, finely chopped
1 small fresh red chilli, seeded and
    finely chopped
115 g/4 oz/generous ½ cup risotto rice
1.2 litres/2 pints/5 cups vegetable stock
salt and freshly ground black pepper
60 ml/4 tbsp grated Pecorino cheese,
    to serve

1 Place the spinach in a large pan with just the water that clings to its leaves after washing. Add a large pinch of salt. Heat gently until the spinach has wilted, then remove from the heat and drain, reserving any liquid. Use a knife to chop finely.

2 Heat the oil in a large saucepan and cook the onion, garlic and chilli for 4–5 minutes until softened. Stir in the rice until well coated, then pour in the stock and reserved spinach liquid.

3 Bring to the boil, lower the heat and simmer for 10 minutes. Add the spinach and cook for 5–7 minutes more, until the rice is tender. Season with salt and freshly ground pepper and serve with the Pecorino cheese.

Broccoli, Anchovy and Pasta Soup

This soup is from Apulia in the south of Italy, where anchovies and broccoli are often used together.

INGREDIENTS

Serves 4

30 ml/2 tbsp olive oil
1 small onion, finely chopped
1 garlic clove, finely chopped
¼–⅓ fresh red chilli, seeded and finely
   chopped
2 canned anchovy fillets, drained
200 ml/7 fl oz/scant 1 cup passata
45 ml/3 tbsp dry white wine
1.2 litres/2 pints/5 cups vegetable stock
300 g/11 oz/2 cups broccoli florets
200 g/7 oz/1¾ cups orecchiette
salt and freshly ground black pepper
grated Pecorino cheese, to serve

1 Heat the oil in a large saucepan. Add the onion, garlic, chilli and anchovies and cook over a low heat, stirring all the time, for 5–6 minutes.

2 Add the passata and wine, with salt and pepper to taste. Bring to the boil, cover the pan, then cook over a low heat, stirring occasionally, for 12–15 minutes.

3 Pour in the stock. Bring to the boil, then add the broccoli and simmer for about 5 minutes. Add the pasta and bring back to the boil, stirring. Simmer for 7–8 minutes or according to the instructions on the packet, stirring frequently, until the pasta is *al dente*.

4 Taste and adjust the seasoning. Serve hot, in individual warmed bowls. Hand round the grated Pecorino cheese separately.

Consommé with Agnolotti

Prawns, crab and chicken jostle for the upper hand in this rich and satisfying consommé.

Serves 4–6

75 g/3 oz cooked peeled prawns
75 g/3 oz canned crab meat, drained
5 ml/1 tsp finely grated fresh root ginger
15 ml/l tbsp fresh white breadcrumbs
5 ml/l tsp light soy sauce
1 spring onion, finely chopped
1 garlic clove, crushed
1 egg white, beaten
400 g/14 oz can chicken or fish consommé
30 ml/2 tbsp sherry or vermouth
salt and freshly ground black pepper

For the pasta
200 g/7 oz/1¾ cups plain flour
pinch of salt
2 eggs
10 ml/2 tsp cold water

For the garnish
50 g/2 oz cooked peeled prawns
fresh coriander leaves

1 To make the pasta, sift the flour and salt on to a clean work surface and make a well in the centre with your hand.

2 Put the eggs and water into the well. Using a fork, beat the eggs gently together, then gradually draw in the flour from the sides, to make a thick paste.

3 When the mixture becomes too stiff to use a fork, use your hands to mix to a firm dough. Knead the dough for about 5 minutes until smooth. Wrap in clear film to prevent it drying out and leave to rest for 20-30 minutes.

4 Meanwhile, put the prawns, crab meat, ginger, breadcrumbs, soy sauce, spring onion, garlic and seasoning into a food processor or blender and process until smooth.

5 Once the pasta has rested, roll it into thin sheets. Stamp out 32 rounds 5 cm/2 in in diameter, using a fluted pastry cutter.

6 Place 5 ml/1 tsp of the filling in the centre of half the pasta rounds. Brush the edges of each round with egg white and sandwich with a second round on top. Pinch the edges together to stop the filling seeping out.

7 Cook the pasta in a large pan of boiling, salted water for 5 minutes (cook in batches to stop them sticking together). Remove and drop into a bowl of cold water for 5 seconds before placing on a tray. (You can make these pasta shapes a day in advance. Cover with clear film and store in the fridge.)

8 Heat the consommé in a pan with the sherry or vermouth. Add the cooked pasta shapes and simmer for 1–2 minutes.

9 Serve the pasta in soup bowls covered with hot consommé. Garnish with peeled prawns and coriander leaves.

Oyster Soup

Oysters make a delicious soup that is really special.

Serves 6

475 ml/16 fl oz/2 cups milk

475 ml/16 fl oz/2 cups single cream

1.2 litres/2 pints/5 cups shucked oysters, drained, with their liquor reserved

a pinch of paprika

25 g/1 oz/2 tbsp butter

salt and freshly ground black pepper

15 ml/1 tbsp chopped fresh parsley, to garnish

1 Combine the milk, single cream, and oyster liquor in a heavy saucepan.

2 Heat the mixture over medium heat until small bubbles appear around the edge of the pan, being careful not to allow it to boil. Reduce the heat to low and add the oysters.

3 Cook, stirring occasionally, until the oysters plump up and their edges begin to curl. Add the paprika and season to taste.

4 Meanwhile, warm six soup plates or bowls. Cut the butter into 6 pieces and put one piece in each bowl.

Ladle in the oyster soup and sprinkle with chopped parsley. Serve immediately.

Asparagus Soup with Crab

A beautiful, green soup with the pure taste of fresh asparagus. The crab is added at the last moment as a luxurious garnish.

INGREDIENTS

Serves 6–8

1.5 kg/3–3¹⁄₂ lb fresh asparagus
25 g/l oz/2 tbsp butter
1.5 litres/2¹⁄₂ pints/6¹⁄₄ cups chicken stock
30 ml/2 tbsp cornflour
30–45 ml/2–3 tbsp cold water
120 ml/4 fl oz/¹⁄₂ cup whipping cream
salt and freshly ground black pepper
175–200 g/6–7 oz white crab meat,
    to garnish

1 Trim the woody ends from the bottom of the asparagus spears and cut the spears into 2.5 cm/l in pieces.

2 Melt the butter in a heavy saucepan or flameproof casserole over a medium-high heat. Add the asparagus and cook for 5–6 minutes, stirring frequently, until it is bright green, but not browned.

3 Add the stock and bring to the boil over a high heat, skimming off any foam that rises to the surface. Simmer over a medium heat for 3–5 minutes until the asparagus is tender, yet crisp. Reserve 12–16 of the asparagus tips for the garnish. Season the soup, cover and continue cooking for 15–20 minutes until the asparagus is very tender.

4 Purée the soup in a blender or food processor and pass the mixture through the fine blade of a food mill back into the saucepan. Return the soup to the boil over a medium-high heat. Blend the cornflour with the water and whisk into the boiling soup to thicken, then stir in the cream. Adjust the seasoning.

5 To serve, ladle the soup into bowls and top each with a spoonful of the crab meat and a few of the reserved asparagus tips.

Clam and Corn Chowder

Canned or bottled clams in brine, once drained, can be used as an alternative to fresh ones in their shells. Discard any clam shells that remain closed during cooking as this means they were already dead.

INGREDIENTS

Serves 4

300 ml/½ pint/1¼ cups double cream
75 g/3 oz/6 tbsp unsalted butter
1 small onion, finely chopped
1 apple, cored and sliced
1 garlic clove, crushed
45 ml/3 tbsp mild curry powder
350 g/12 oz/3 cups baby sweetcorn
225 g/8 oz cooked new potatoes
24 boiled baby onions
600 ml/1 pint/2½ cups fish stock
40 small clams
salt and freshly ground black pepper
8 lime wedges, to garnish (optional)

3 In another saucepan, melt the remaining butter and add the baby sweetcorn, potatoes and baby onions. Cook for 5 minutes. Increase the heat and add the cream mixture and stock. Bring to the boil.

4 Add the clams. Cover and cook until the clams have opened. Discard any that do not open. Season well to taste with salt and freshly ground black pepper and serve, garnished with lime wedges, if liked.

1 Pour the cream into a small saucepan and cook over a high heat until it is reduced by half.

2 In a larger pan, melt half the butter. Add the onion, apple, garlic and curry powder. Sauté until the onion is translucent. Add the reduced cream and stir well.

Saffron Mussel Soup

*This is one of France's most delicious
seafood soups. For everyday eating,
the French would normally serve all
the mussels in their shells. Serve
with plenty of French bread.*

INGREDIENTS

Serves 4–6

40 g/1½ oz/3 tbsp unsalted butter
8 shallots, finely chopped
1 bouquet garni
5 ml/1 tsp black peppercorns
350 ml/12 fl oz/l½ cups dry white wine
1 kg/2¼ lb mussels, scrubbed and
    debearded
2 medium leeks, trimmed and finely
    chopped
1 fennel bulb, finely chopped
1 carrot, finely chopped
several saffron strands
1 litre/1¾ pints/4 cups fish or chicken
    stock
30–45 ml/2–3 tbsp cornflour, blended
    with 45 ml/3 tbsp cold water
120 ml/4 fl oz/½ cup whipping cream
1 medium tomato, peeled, seeded and
    finely chopped
30 ml/2 tbsp Pernod (optional)
salt and freshly ground black pepper

1 In a large, heavy pan, melt half
the butter over a medium-
high heat. Add half the shallots
and cook for 1–2 minutes until
softened but not coloured. Add the
bouquet garni, peppercorns and
white wine and bring to the boil.
Add the mussels, cover tightly
and cook over a high heat for
3–5 minutes, shaking the pan from
time to time, until the mussels
have opened.

2 With a slotted spoon, transfer
the mussels to a bowl. Strain
the cooking liquid through a
muslin-lined sieve and reserve.

3 Pull open the shells and
remove most of the mussels.
Discard any closed mussels.

4 Melt the remaining butter
over a medium heat. Add the
remaining shallots and cook for
1–2 minutes. Add the leeks, fennel,
carrot and saffron and cook for
3–5 minutes.

5 Stir in the reserved cooking
liquid, bring to the boil and
cook for 5 minutes until the
vegetables are tender and the
liquid is slightly reduced. Add
the stock and bring to the boil,
skimming any foam that rises
to the surface. Season with salt,
if needed, and black pepper and
cook for a further 5 minutes.

6 Stir the blended cornflour
into the soup. Simmer for
2–3 minutes until the soup is
slightly thickened, then add the
cream, mussels and chopped
tomato. Stir in the Pernod, if
using, cook for 1–2 minutes until
hot, then serve immediately.

Seafood Wonton Soup

This is a variation on the popular wonton soup that is traditionally prepared using pork.

Serves 4

50 g/2 oz raw tiger prawns
50 g/2 oz queen scallops
75 g/3 oz skinless cod fillet, roughly chopped
15 ml/1 tbsp finely snipped fresh chives
5 ml/1 tsp dry sherry
1 small egg white, lightly beaten
2.5 ml/½ tsp sesame oil
1.5 ml/¼ tsp salt
large pinch of ground white pepper
20 wonton wrappers
2 cos lettuce leaves, shredded
900 ml/1½ pints/3¾ cups fish stock
fresh coriander leaves and garlic chives, to garnish

1 Peel and devein the prawns. Rinse, dry on kitchen paper and cut into small pieces.

2 Rinse and dry the scallops. Chop them into small pieces the same size as the prawns.

3 Place the cod in a food processor and process until a paste is formed. Scrape into a bowl and stir in the prawns, scallops, chives, sherry, egg white, sesame oil, salt and pepper. Mix well, cover and leave in a cool place to marinate for 20 minutes.

4 Make the wontons. Place 5 ml/1 tsp of the seafood filling in the centre of a wonton wrapper, then bring the corners together to meet at the top. Twist them together to enclose the filling. Fill the remaining wonton wrappers in the same way. Tie with a fresh chive if desired.

COOK'S TIP

The filled wonton wrappers can be made ahead, then frozen for several weeks and cooked straight from the freezer.

5 Bring a large saucepan of water to the boil. Drop in the wontons. When the water returns to the boil, lower the heat and simmer gently for 5 minutes or until the wontons float to the surface. Drain the wontons and divide them among four heated soup bowls.

6 Add a portion of lettuce to each bowl. Bring the fish stock to the boil. Ladle it on top of the lettuce and garnish each portion with coriander leaves and garlic chives. Serve immediately.

Lobster Bisque

The blue and black clawed lobster is known as the king of the shellfish. When cooked, it turns brilliant red in colour. This is an extravagant soup, worthy of a celebration dinner party.

INGREDIENTS

Serves 4

1 cooked lobster (about 675 g/1½ lb)
30 ml/2 tbsp vegetable oil
115 g/4 oz/½ cup butter
2 shallots, finely chopped
juice of ½ lemon
45 ml/3 tbsp brandy
1 bay leaf
1 sprig of fresh parsley, plus extra
    to garnish
1 blade of mace
1.2 litres/2 pints/5 cups fish stock
40 g/1½ oz/3 tbsp plain flour
45 ml/3 tbsp double cream
salt and freshly ground black pepper
a pinch of cayenne pepper, to garnish

1 Preheat the oven to 180°C/ 350°F/Gas 4. Lay the lobster out flat and split in half lengthways. Remove and discard the little stomach sac from the head, the thread-like intestine and the coral (if any).

2 In a large, heavy-based roasting tin, heat the oil with 25 g/1 oz/2 tbsp of the butter. Sauté the lobster, flesh-side down, for 5 minutes. Add the shallots, lemon juice and brandy, then cook in the oven for 15 minutes.

3 Remove the lobster meat from the shell. Place the shell and the juices in a large saucepan and simmer with the bay leaf, parsley, mace and stock for 30 minutes. Strain. Finely chop 15 ml/1 tbsp of the lobster meat. Process the rest with 40 g/1½ oz/3 tbsp of the butter.

4 Melt the remaining butter, add the flour and cook gently for 30 seconds. Add the stock gradually and bring to the boil, stirring constantly. Stir in the processed meat, the cream and seasoning.

5 Ladle into individual serving dishes and garnish with chopped lobster, parsley sprigs and a sprinkling of cayenne.

Prawn and Egg-knot Soup

An unusual and special soup, just right for a festive occasion.

INGREDIENTS

Serves 4

900 ml/1½ pints/3¾ cups kombu and
    bonito stock or instant dashi
5 ml/1 tsp soy sauce
a dash of sake or dry white wine
salt
1 spring onion, finely sliced, to garnish

For the prawn shinjo balls
200 g/7 oz raw large prawns, shelled,
    thawed if frozen
65 g/2½ oz cod fillet, skinned
5 ml/1 tsp egg white
5 ml/1 tsp sake or dry white wine
22.5 ml/4½ tsp cornflour or potato starch
2–3 drops of soy sauce

For the omelette
1 egg, beaten
a dash of mirin
oil, for frying

1 Devein the prawns. Process the prawns, cod, egg white, 5 ml/1 tsp sake or wine, cornflour or potato starch, soy sauce and a pinch of salt in a food processor or blender to make a sticky paste. Alternatively, finely chop the prawns and cod, crush them with the knife's blade and then pound them well in a mortar with a pestle, before adding the remaining ingredients.

2 Shape the mixture into four balls and steam them for 10 minutes over a high heat. Meanwhile, soak the spring onion for the garnish in cold water for 5 minutes, then drain.

3 To make the omelette, mix the egg with a pinch of salt and the mirin. Heat a little oil in a frying pan and pour in the egg, tilting the pan to coat it evenly. When the egg has set, turn the omelette over and cook for 30 seconds. Leave to cool.

4 Cut the omelette into long strips about 2 cm/¾ in wide. Knot each strip once, place in a sieve and rinse with hot water to remove excess oil. Bring the stock or dashi to the boil and add the soy sauce, a pinch of salt and a dash of sake or wine. Divide the prawn balls and the egg knots among four bowls. Pour in the soup, sprinkle with the spring onion and serve.

Thai Fish Soup

Thai fish sauce, or nam pla, *is rich in B vitamins and is used extensively in Thai cooking. It is available at Thai or Indonesian shops and good supermarkets.*

INGREDIENTS

Serves 4

350 g/12 oz raw large prawns

15 ml/1 tbsp groundnut oil

1.2 litres/2 pints/5 cups well-flavoured chicken or fish stock

1 lemon grass stalk, bruised and cut into 2.5 cm/1 in lengths

2 kaffir lime leaves, torn into pieces

juice and finely grated rind of 1 lime

1/2 fresh green chilli, seeded and finely sliced

4 scallops

24 mussels, scrubbed

115 g/4 oz monkfish fillet, cut into 2 cm/3/4 in chunks

10 ml/2 tsp nam pla

For the garnish

1 kaffir lime leaf, shredded

1/2 fresh red chilli, finely sliced

1 Peel the prawns, reserving the shells, and remove the black vein running along their backs.

2 Heat the oil in a saucepan and fry the prawn shells until pink. Add the stock, lemon grass, lime leaves, lime rind and green chilli. Bring to the boil, simmer for 20 minutes, then strain through a sieve, reserving the liquid.

3 Prepare the scallops by cutting them in half, leaving the corals attached to one half.

4 Return the stock to a clean pan, add the prawns, mussels, monkfish and scallops and cook for 3 minutes. Remove from the heat and add the lime juice and nam pla.

5 Serve garnished with the shredded lime leaf and finely sliced red chilli.

Seafarer's Stew

Any variety of firm fish may be used in this recipe, but be sure to use smoked haddock as well; it is essential for its distinctive flavour.

INGREDIENTS

Serves 4

225 g/8 oz undyed smoked haddock fillet

225 g/8 oz fresh monkfish fillet

20 mussels, scrubbed

2 streaky bacon rashers (optional)

15 ml/1 tbsp olive oil

1 shallot, finely chopped

225 g/8 oz carrots, coarsely grated

150 ml/¼ pint/⅔ cup single or double cream

115 g/4 oz cooked peeled prawns

salt and freshly ground black pepper

30 ml/2 tbsp chopped fresh parsley, to garnish

1 In a large, heavy-based pan, simmer the haddock and monkfish in 1.2 litres/2 pints/ 5 cups water for 5 minutes, then add the mussels and cover the pan with a lid.

2 Cook for a further 5 minutes or until all the mussels have opened. Discard any that have not. Drain, reserving the liquid. Return the liquid to the rinsed pan and set aside.

3 Flake the haddock coarsely, removing any skin and bones, then cut the monkfish into large chunks. Cut the bacon, if using, into strips.

4 Heat the oil in a heavy-based frying pan and fry the shallot and bacon for 3–4 minutes or until the shallot is soft and the bacon lightly browned. Add to the strained fish broth, bring to the boil, then add the grated carrots and cook for 10 minutes.

5 Stir in the cream together with the haddock, monkfish, mussels and prawns and heat gently, without boiling. Season and serve in large bowls, garnished with parsley.

Corn and Crab Bisque

This is a Louisiana classic, which is certainly luxurious enough for a dinner party and is therefore well worth the extra time required to prepare the fresh crab. The crab shells, together with the corn cobs, from which the kernels are stripped, make a fine-flavoured stock.

INGREDIENTS

Serves 8

4 large sweetcorn cobs
2 bay leaves
1 cooked crab (about 1 kg/2¼ lb)
25 g/1 oz/2 tbsp butter
30 ml/2 tbsp plain flour
300 ml/½ pint/1¼ cups whipping cream
6 spring onions, shredded
a pinch of cayenne pepper
salt and freshly ground black and
    white pepper
hot French bread or grissini breadsticks,
    to serve

1 Pull away the husks and silk from the cobs of corn and strip off the kernels.

2 Keep the kernels on one side and put the stripped cobs into a deep saucepan or flameproof casserole with 3 litres/5 pints/ 12½ cups cold water, the bay leaves and 10 ml/2 tsp salt. Bring to the boil and leave to simmer while you prepare the crab.

3 Pull away the two flaps between the big claws of the crab, stand it on its "nose", where the flaps were, and bang down firmly with the heel of your hand on the rounded end.

4 Separate the crab from its top shell, keeping the shell.

5 Push out the crab's mouth and its abdominal sac immediately below the mouth, and discard.

6 Pull away the feathery gills surrounding the central chamber and discard. Scrape out all the semi-liquid brown meat from the shell and set aside.

7 Crack the claws in as many places as necessary to extract all the white meat. Pick out the white meat from the fragile cavities in the central body of the crab. Set aside all the crab meat, brown and white. Put the spidery legs, back shell and all the other pieces of shell into the pan with the corn cobs. Simmer for a further 15 minutes, then strain the stock into a clean pan and boil hard to reduce to 2 litres/3½ pints/9 cups.

8 Meanwhile, melt the butter in a small pan and sprinkle in the flour. Stir constantly over a low heat until the roux is the colour of rich cream.

9 Off the heat, slowly stir in 250 ml/8 fl oz/1 cup of the stock. Return to the heat and stir until it thickens, then stir this thickened mixture into the pan of strained stock.

10 Add the corn kernels, return to the boil and simmer for 5 minutes.

11 Add the crab meat, cream and spring onions and season with cayenne, salt and pepper (preferably a mixture of black and white). Return to the boil and simmer for a further 2 minutes. Serve with hot French bread or grissini breadsticks.

Seafood Soup with Rouille

This is a really chunky, aromatic mixed fish soup from France, flavoured with plenty of saffron and herbs. Rouille, a fiery hot paste, is served separately for everyone to swirl into their soup to flavour.

INGREDIENTS

Serves 6

3 gurnard or red mullet, scaled and gutted

12 large prawns

675 g/1½ lb white fish, such as cod, haddock, halibut or monkfish

225 g/8 oz mussels

1 onion, quartered

1.2 litres/2 pints/5 cups water

5 ml/1 tsp saffron strands

75 ml/5 tbsp olive oil

1 fennel bulb, roughly chopped

4 garlic cloves, crushed

3 strips pared orange rind

4 sprigs of thyme

675 g/1½ lb tomatoes or 400 g/14 oz can chopped tomatoes

30 ml/2 tbsp sun-dried tomato purée

3 bay leaves

salt and freshly ground black pepper

For the rouille

1 red pepper, seeded and roughly chopped

1 fresh red chilli, seeded and sliced

2 garlic cloves, chopped

75 ml/5 tbsp olive oil

15 g/½ oz/¼ cup fresh breadcrumbs

1 To make the *rouille*, process the pepper, chilli, garlic, oil and breadcrumbs in a blender or food processor until smooth. Transfer to a serving dish and chill.

2 Fillet the gurnard or mullet by cutting away the flesh from the backbone. Reserve the heads and bones. Cut the fillets into small chunks. Shell half the prawns and reserve the trimmings to make the stock. Skin the white fish, discarding any bones, and cut into large chunks. Scrub the mussels well, discarding any open ones.

3 Put the fish trimmings and prawn trimmings in a saucepan with the onion and water. Bring to the boil, then simmer gently for 30 minutes. Cool slightly and strain.

4 Soak the saffron in 15 ml/ 1 tbsp boiling water. Heat 30 ml/2 tbsp of the oil in a large sauté pan or saucepan. Add the gurnard or mullet and white fish and fry over a high heat for 1 minute. Drain.

5 Heat the remaining oil and fry the fennel, garlic, orange rind and thyme until beginning to colour. Make up the strained stock to about 1.2 litres/2 pints/5 cups with water.

6 If using fresh tomatoes, plunge them into boiling water for 30 seconds, then refresh in cold water. Peel and chop. Add the stock to the pan with the saffron, tomatoes, tomato purée and bay leaves. Season, bring almost to the boil, then simmer gently, covered, for 20 minutes.

7 Stir in the gurnard or mullet, white fish, shelled and non-shelled prawns and add the mussels. Cover the pan and cook for 3–4 minutes. Discard any mussels that do not open. Serve the soup hot with the *rouille*.

COOK'S TIP

To save time, order the fish and ask the fishmonger to fillet the gurnard or mullet for you.

Creamy Cod Chowder

The sharp flavour of the smoked cod contrasts well with the creamy soup. Serve this soup as a substantial starter before a light main course. Warm, crusty wholemeal bread goes well with it.

INGREDIENTS

Serves 4–6

350 g/12 oz smoked cod fillet
1 small onion, finely chopped
1 bay leaf
4 black peppercorns
900 ml/1½ pints/3¾ cups milk
10 ml/2 tsp cornflour
10 ml/2 tsp cold water
200 g/7 oz can sweetcorn kernels
15 ml/1 tbsp chopped fresh parsley
crusty wholemeal bread, to serve

COOK'S TIP

The flavour of the chowder improves if it is made a day in advance. Chill in the refrigerator until required, then reheat gently to prevent the fish from disintegrating.

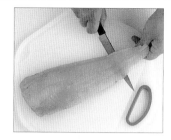

1 Skin the fish with a knife and put into a large saucepan with the onion, bay leaf, black peppercorns and milk.

2 Bring to the boil. Reduce the heat and simmer very gently for 12–15 minutes, or until the fish is just cooked. Do not overcook.

3 Using a slotted spoon, lift out the fish and flake into large chunks. Remove and discard the bay leaf and peppercorns.

4 Blend the cornflour with the water carefully until it forms a smooth paste, and add to the saucepan. Bring to the boil and simmer for 1 minute or until slightly thickened.

5 Drain the sweetcorn kernels and add to the saucepan together with the flaked fish and chopped fresh parsley.

6 Reheat the soup until piping hot, but do not boil, taking care that the fish does not disintegrate. Ladle into soup bowls and serve straight away with plenty of warm wholemeal bread.

Clam and Basil Soup

Subtly sweet and spicy, this soup is an ideal starter for serving as part of a celebration dinner.

INGREDIENTS

Serves 4–6

30 ml/2 tbsp olive oil
1 medium onion, finely chopped
leaves from 1 fresh or dried sprig of
    thyme, chopped or crumbled
2 garlic cloves, crushed
5–6 fresh basil leaves, plus extra to garnish
1.5–2.5 ml/¼–½ tsp crushed red chillies,
    to taste
1 litre/1¾ pints/4 cups fish stock
350 ml/12 fl oz/1½ cups passata
5 ml/1 tsp granulated sugar
90 g/3½ oz/scant 1 cup frozen peas
65 g/2½ oz/⅔ cup small pasta shapes,
    such as chifferini
225 g/8 oz frozen shelled clams
salt and freshly ground black pepper

1 Heat the oil in a large saucepan, add the onion and cook gently for about 5 minutes until softened but not coloured. Add the thyme, then stir in the garlic, basil leaves and chillies.

2 Add the stock, passata and sugar to the saucepan, with salt and pepper to taste. Bring to the boil, then lower the heat and simmer gently for 15 minutes, stirring from time to time. Add the frozen peas and cook for a further 5 minutes.

3 Add the pasta to the stock mixture and bring to the boil, stirring. Lower the heat and simmer for about 5 minutes or according to the packet instructions, stirring frequently, until the pasta is *al dente*.

4 Turn the heat down to low, add the frozen clams and heat through for 2–3 minutes. Taste and adjust the seasoning. Serve hot in warmed bowls, garnished with basil leaves.

COOK'S TIP

Frozen shelled clams are available at good fishmongers and supermarkets. If you can't get them, use bottled or canned clams in natural juice (not vinegar). Italian delicatessens sell jars of clams in their shells. These both look and taste delicious and are not too expensive. For a special occasion, stir some into the soup.

Pasta Soup with Chicken Livers

A soup that can be served as a first or main course. The fried chicken livers are so delicious that, even if you do not normally like them, you will find yourself lapping them up in this soup.

Serves 4–6

115 g/4 oz/½ cup chicken livers, thawed
   if frozen
15 ml/1 tbsp olive oil
a knob of butter
4 garlic cloves, crushed
3 sprigs each of fresh parsley, marjoram
   and sage, chopped
1 sprig of fresh thyme, chopped
5–6 fresh basil leaves, chopped
15–30 ml/1–2 tbsp dry white wine
2 x 300 g/11 oz cans condensed
   chicken consommé
225 g/8 oz/2 cups frozen peas
50 g/2 oz/½ cup small pasta shapes, such
   as farfalle
2–3 spring onions, sliced diagonally
salt and freshly ground black pepper

1 Cut the chicken livers into small pieces with scissors. Heat the oil and butter in a frying pan, add the garlic and herbs, with salt and ground black pepper to taste, and fry gently for a few minutes. Add the livers, increase the heat to high and stir-fry for a few minutes until they change colour and become dry. Add the wine, cook until it evaporates, then remove from the heat.

2 Tip both cans of chicken consommé into a large saucepan and add water to the condensed soup as directed on the labels. Add an extra can of water, then stir in a little salt and pepper to taste and bring to the boil.

3 Add the frozen peas to the pan and simmer for about 5 minutes, then add the small pasta shapes and bring the soup back to the boil, stirring. Allow to simmer, stirring frequently, for about 5 minutes or according to the instructions on the packet, until the pasta is *al dente*.

4 Add the fried chicken livers and spring onions and heat through for 2–3 minutes. Taste and adjust the seasoning. Serve hot, in warmed bowls.

Ginger, Chicken and Coconut Soup

This aromatic soup is rich with coconut milk and intensely flavoured with galangal, lemon grass and kaffir lime leaves.

INGREDIENTS

Serves 4–6

750 ml/1¼ pints/3 cups coconut milk

475 ml/16 fl oz/2 cups chicken stock

4 lemon grass stalks, bruised and chopped

2.5 cm/1 in piece galangal, finely sliced

10 black peppercorns, crushed

10 kaffir lime leaves, torn

300 g/11 oz skinless boneless chicken, cut
    into thin strips

115 g/4 oz button mushrooms

50 g/2 oz/½ cup baby sweetcorn

60 ml/4 tbsp lime juice

45 ml/3 tbsp fish sauce

For the garnish

2 red chillies, chopped

3–4 spring onions, chopped

chopped fresh coriander

1 Bring the coconut milk and chicken stock to the boil in a saucepan. Add the lemon grass, galangal, peppercorns and half the kaffir lime leaves, reduce the heat and simmer gently for 10 minutes.

2 Strain the stock into a clean pan. Return to the heat, then add the chicken, mushrooms and baby sweetcorn. Cook for about 5–7 minutes until the chicken is cooked.

3 Stir in the lime juice, fish sauce to taste and the rest of the lime leaves. Serve hot, garnished with red chillies, spring onions and coriander.

Indian Beef and Berry Soup

*The fresh berries give this soup a
pleasant kick.*

INGREDIENTS

Serves 4

30 ml/2 tbsp vegetable oil

450 g/1 lb tender beef steak

2 medium onions, finely sliced

25 g/1 oz/2 tbsp butter

1 litre/1¾ pints/4 cups good beef stock or
  bouillon

2.5 ml/½ tsp salt

115 g/4 oz/1 cup fresh huckleberries, blue-
  berries or blackberries, lightly mashed

15 ml/1 tbsp honey

1 Heat the oil in a heavy-based
  saucepan until almost
smoking. Add the steak and brown
on both sides over a medium-high
heat. Remove the steak from the
pan and set aside.

2 Reduce the heat to low and
  add the sliced onions and
butter to the pan. Stir well,
scraping up the meat juices. Cook
over a low heat for 8–10 minutes
until the onions are softened.

3 Add the beef stock or bouillon
  and salt and bring to the boil,
stirring well. Mix in the mashed
berries and the honey. Simmer for
20 minutes.

4 Meanwhile, cut the steak into
  thin, bite-size slivers. Taste the
soup and add more salt or honey
if necessary. Add the steak to the
pan. Cook gently for 30 seconds,
stirring all the time, then serve.

Index

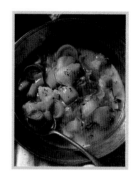

NOTES

NOTES

NOTES

NOTES

NOTES

NOTES

NOTES

NOTES